# the battles of bridget lee

# INVASION OF FARFALL

*E— 2016*

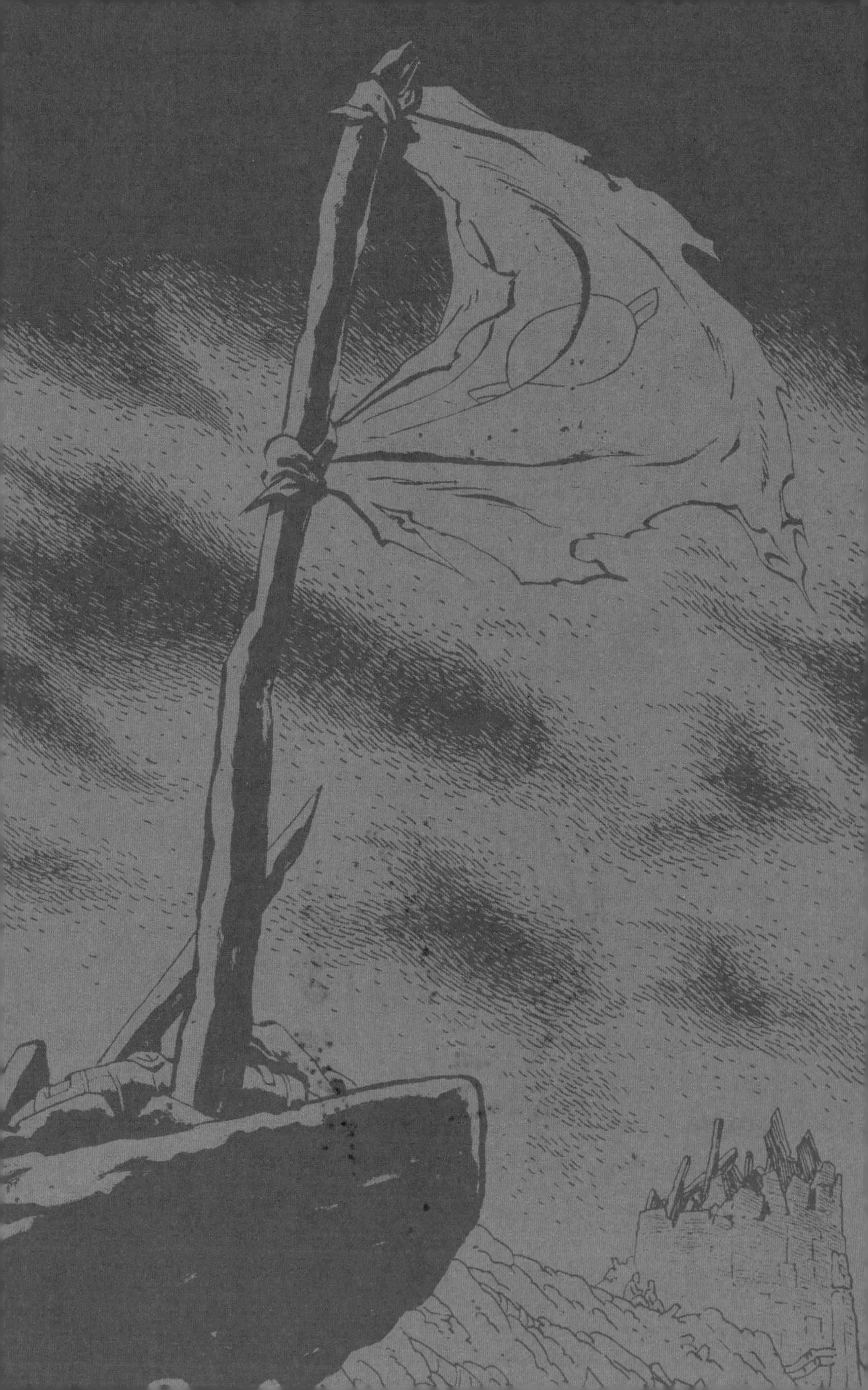

# the battles of bridget lee

## INVASION OF FARFALL

### ETHAN YOUNG

DARK HORSE BOOKS

President & Publisher
**MIKE RICHARDSON**

Editor
**SPENCER CUSHING**

Assistant Editor
**KEVIN BURKHALTER**

Designer
**BRENNAN THOME**

Digital Art Technician
**CHRISTIANNE GOUDREAU**

*Special thanks to Jim Gibbons, Sierra Hahn, Jon Haeffner,*
*Spencer Cushing, and Carol Jean Huang (my wife).—EY*

DarkHorse.com

First edition: September 2016
ISBN 978-1-50670-012-0
10 9 8 7 6 5 4 3 2 1
Printed in China

Published by Dark Horse Books
A division of Dark Horse Comics, Inc.
10956 SE Main Street
Milwaukie, OR 97222

**THE BATTLES OF BRIDGET LEE: INVASION OF FARFALL**

NEIL HANKERSON Executive Vice President TOM WEDDLE Chief Financial Officer RANDY STRADLEY Vice President of Publishing MICHAEL MARTENS Vice President of Book Trade Sales MATT PARKINSON Vice President of Marketing DAVID SCROGGY Vice President of Product Development DALE LAFOUNTAIN Vice President of Information Technology CARA NIECE Vice President of Production and Scheduling NICK McWHORTER Vice President of Media Licensing KEN LIZZI General Counsel DAVE MARSHALL Editor in Chief DAVEY ESTRADA Editorial Director SCOTT ALLIE Executive Senior Editor CHRIS WARNER Senior Books Editor CARY GRAZZINI Director of Print and Development LIA RIBACCHI Art Director MARK BERNARDI Director of Digital Publishing MICHAEL GOMBOS Director of International Publishing and Licensing

To find a comics shop in your area, call the Comic Shop Locator Service toll-free at (888) 266-4226.

International Licensing: 503-905-2377

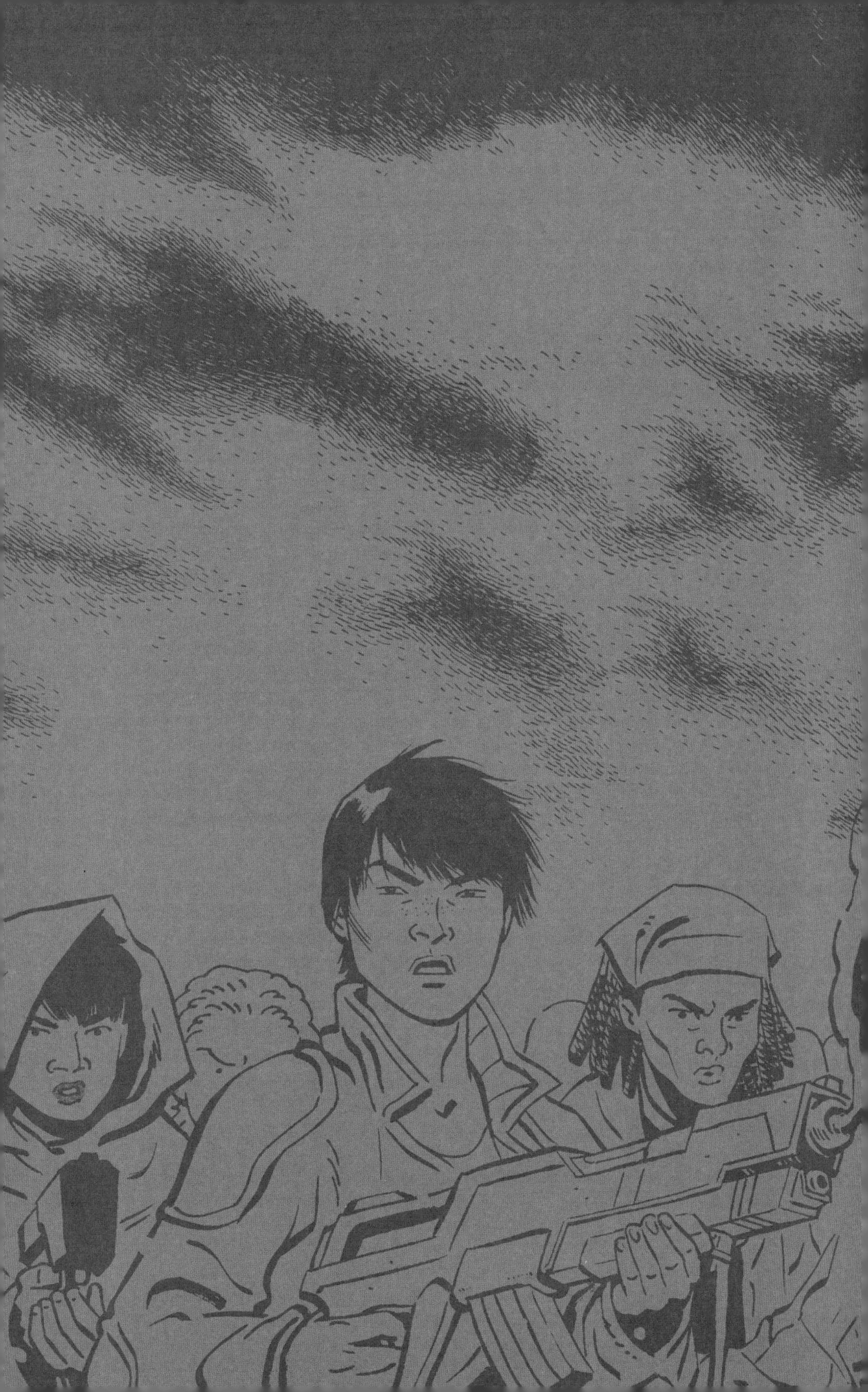

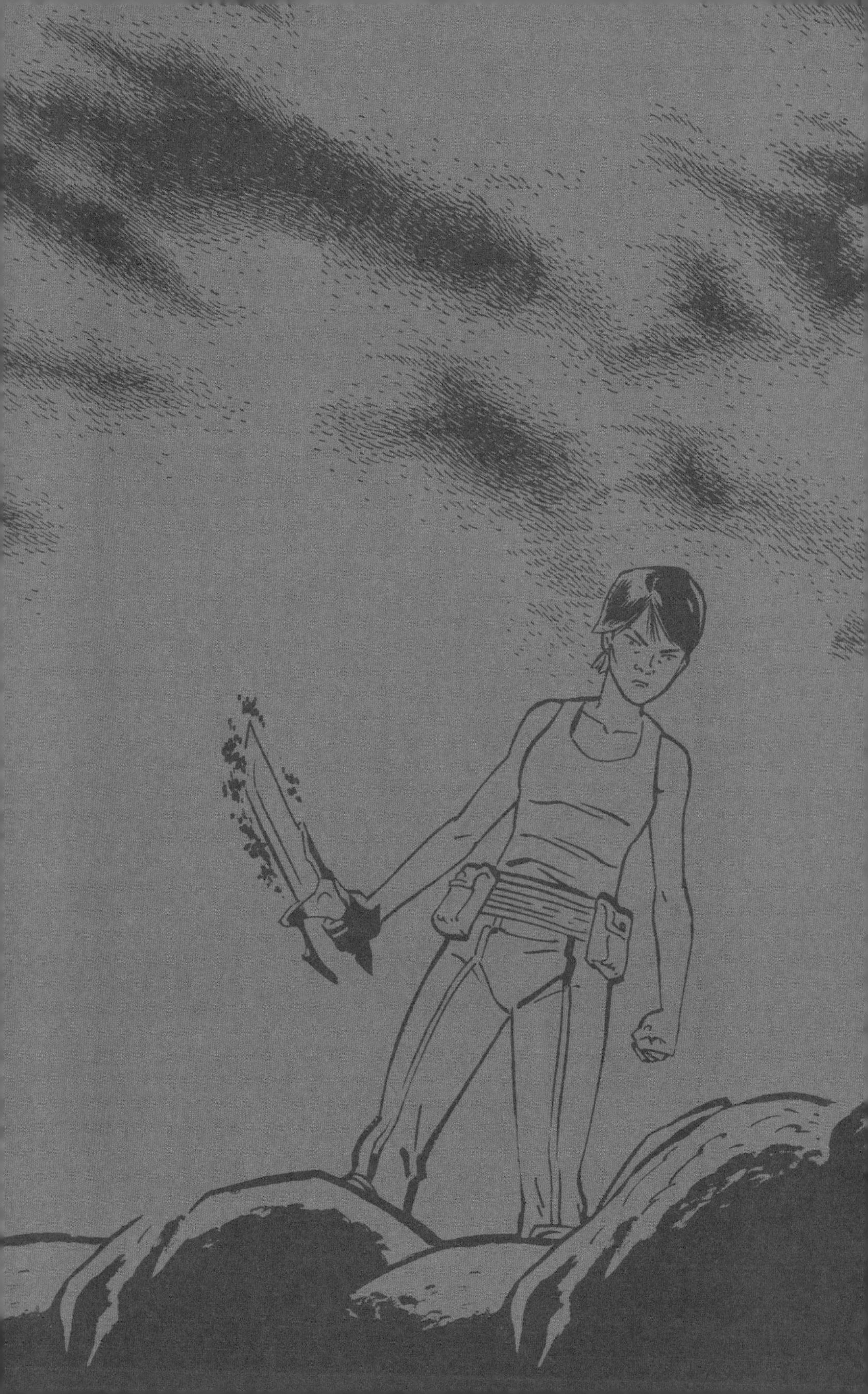

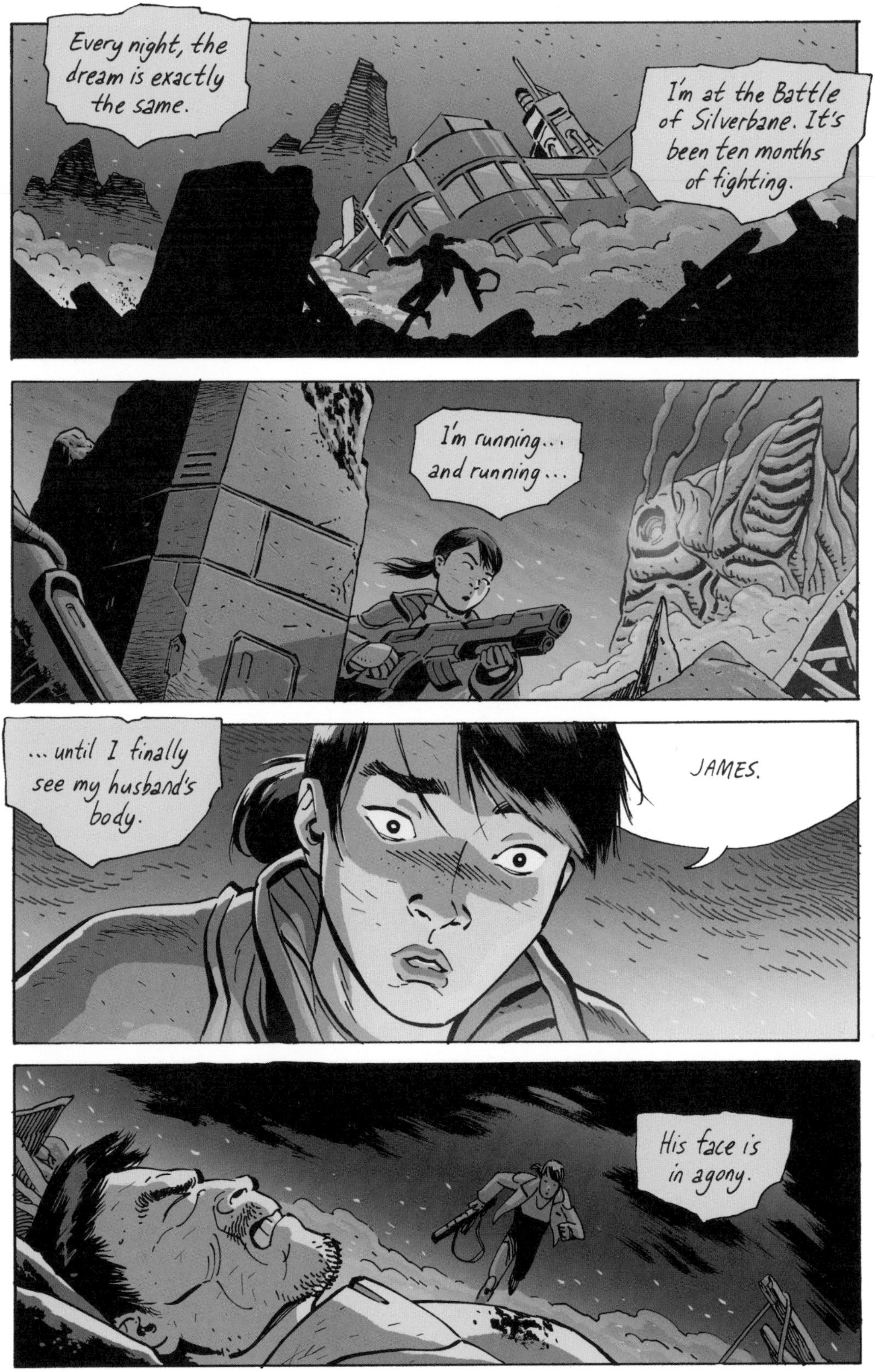
Every night, the dream is exactly the same.
I'm at the Battle of Silverbane. It's been ten months of fighting.
I'm running... and running...
... until I finally see my husband's body.
JAMES.
His face is in agony.

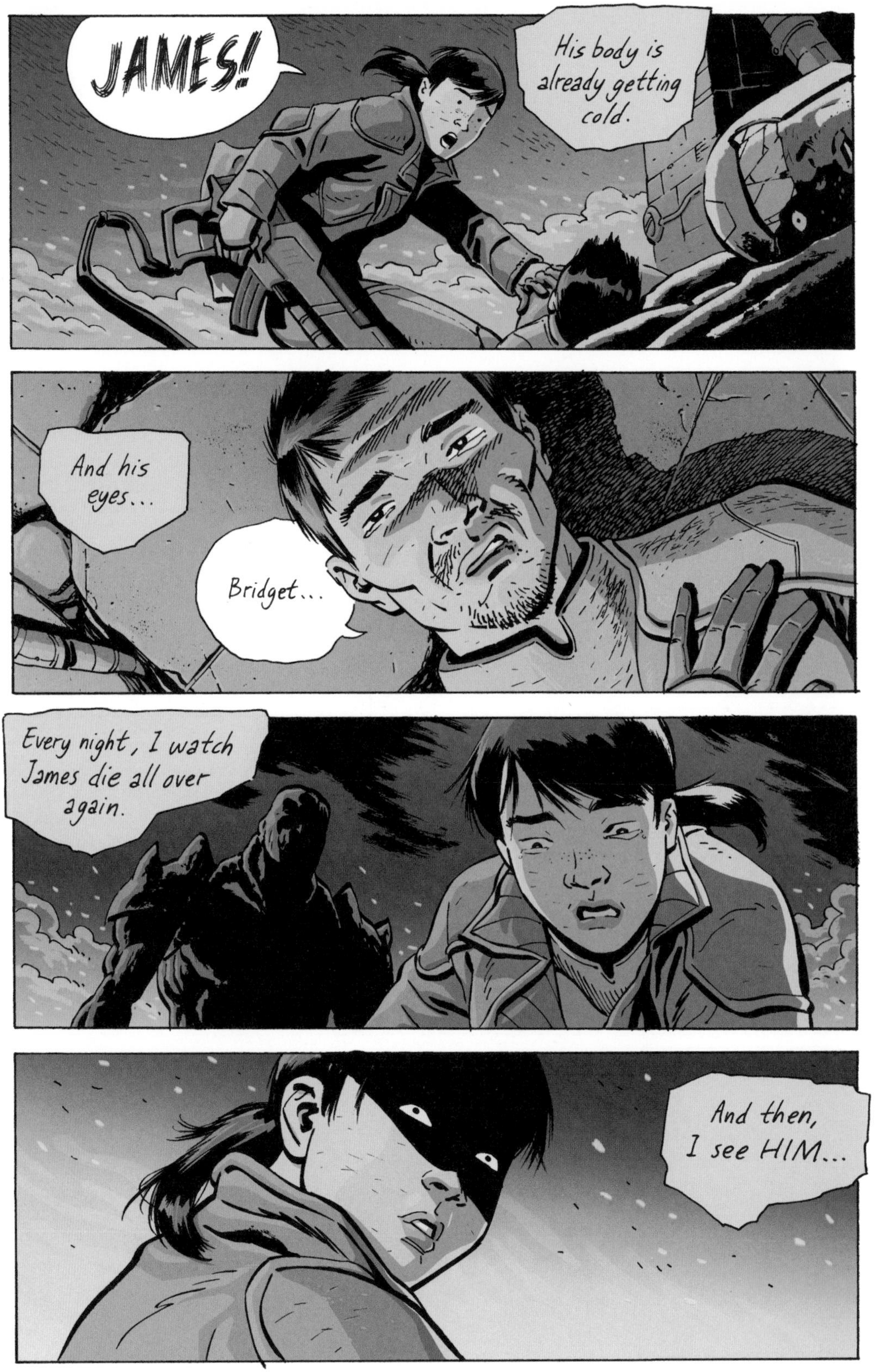
JAMES!
His body is already getting cold.
And his eyes...
Bridget...
Every night, I watch James die all over again.
And then, I see HIM...

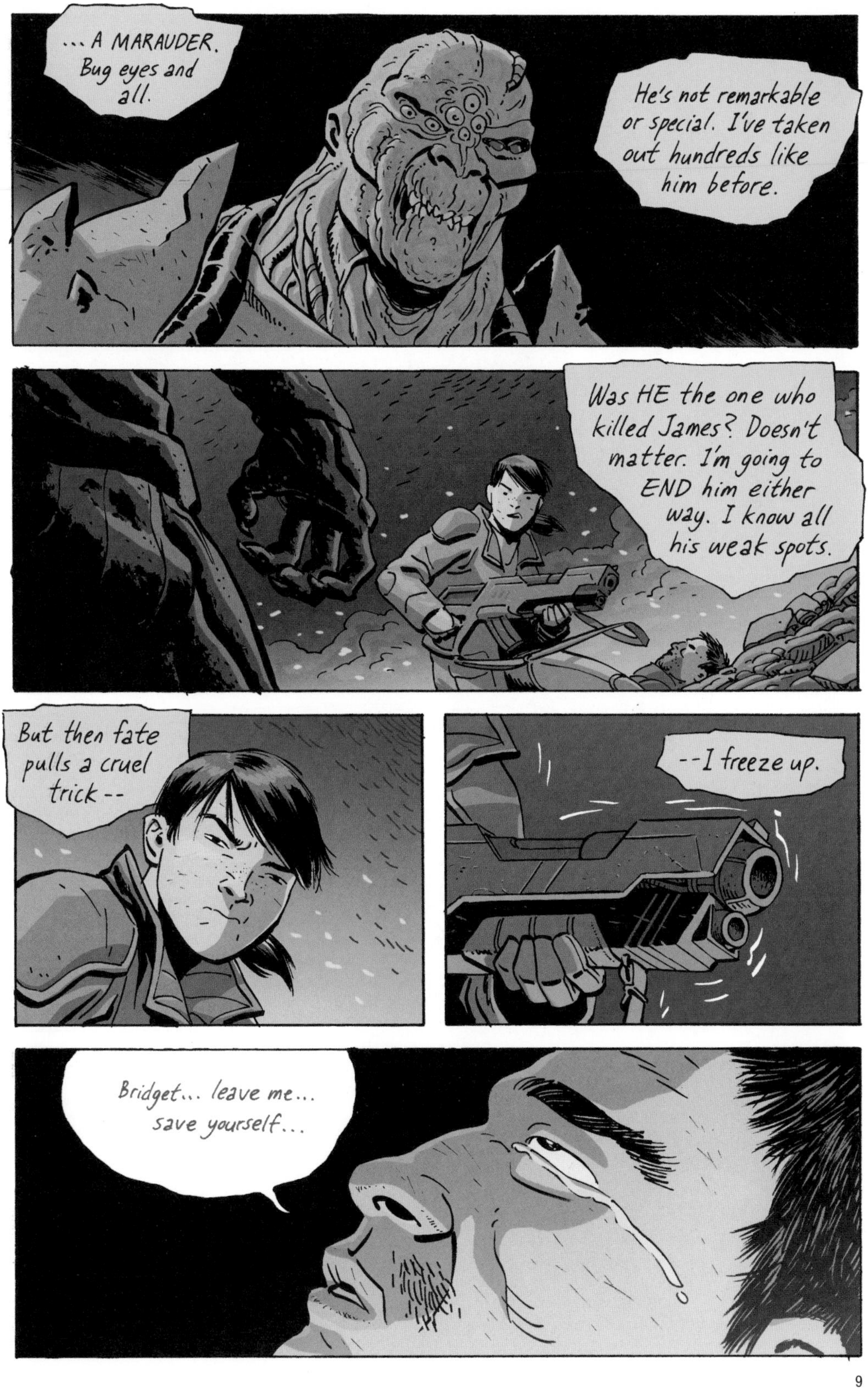
...A MARAUDER. Bug eyes and all.
He's not remarkable or special. I've taken out hundreds like him before.
Was HE the one who killed James? Doesn't matter. I'm going to END him either way. I know all his weak spots.
But then fate pulls a cruel trick--
--I freeze up.
Bridget... leave me... save yourself...

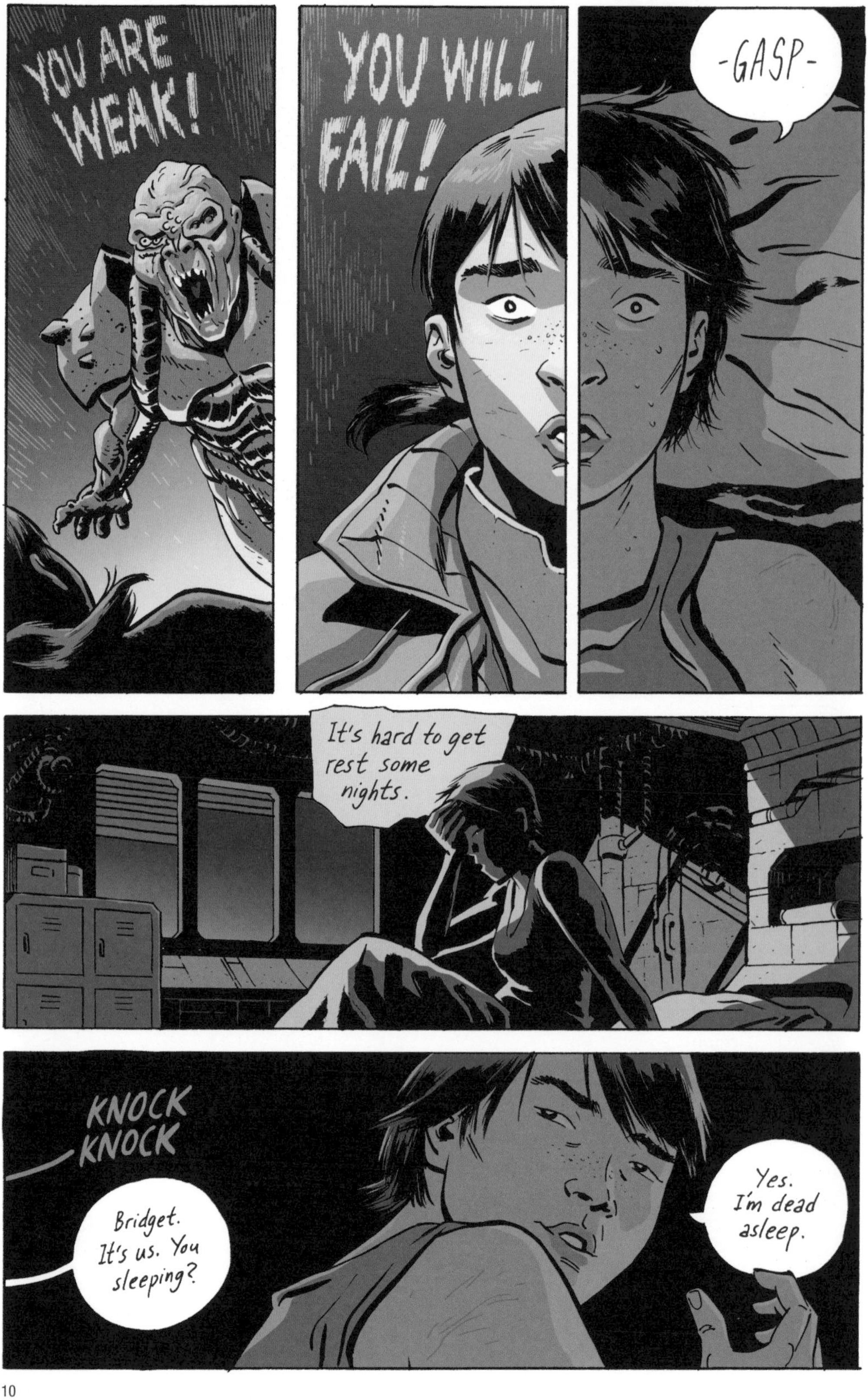
YOU ARE WEAK!
YOU WILL FAIL!
-GASP-
It's hard to get rest some nights.
KNOCK KNOCK
Bridget. It's us. You sleeping?
Yes. I'm dead asleep.

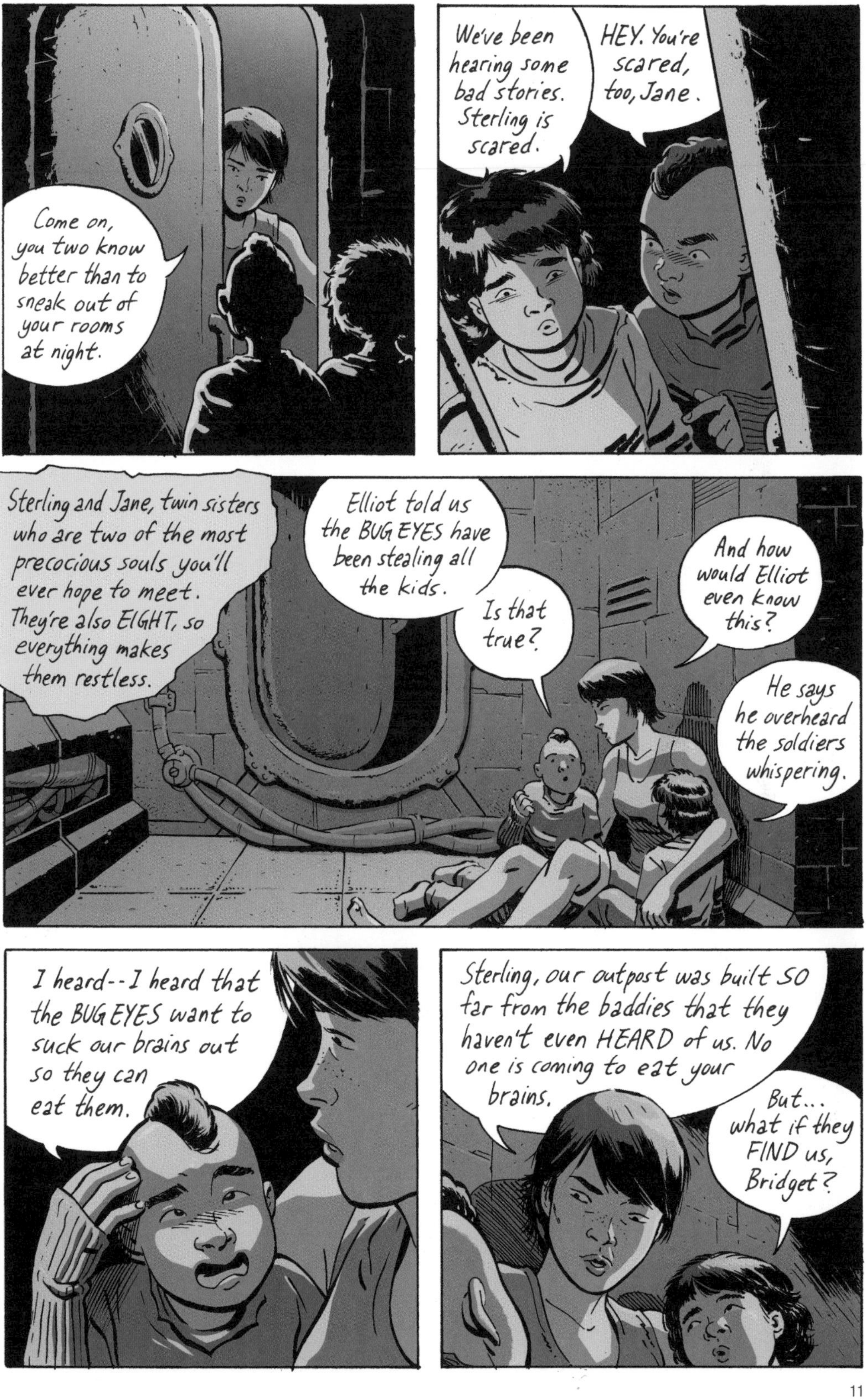
Come on, you two know better than to sneak out of your rooms at night.
We've been hearing some bad stories. Sterling is scared.
HEY. You're scared, too, Jane.
Sterling and Jane, twin sisters who are two of the most precocious souls you'll ever hope to meet. They're also EIGHT, so everything makes them restless.
Elliot told us the BUG EYES have been stealing all the kids.
Is that true?
And how would Elliot even know this?
He says he overheard the soldiers whispering.
I heard--I heard that the BUG EYES want to suck our brains out so they can eat them.
Sterling, our outpost was built SO far from the baddies that they haven't even HEARD of us. No one is coming to eat your brains.
But... what if they FIND us, Bridget?

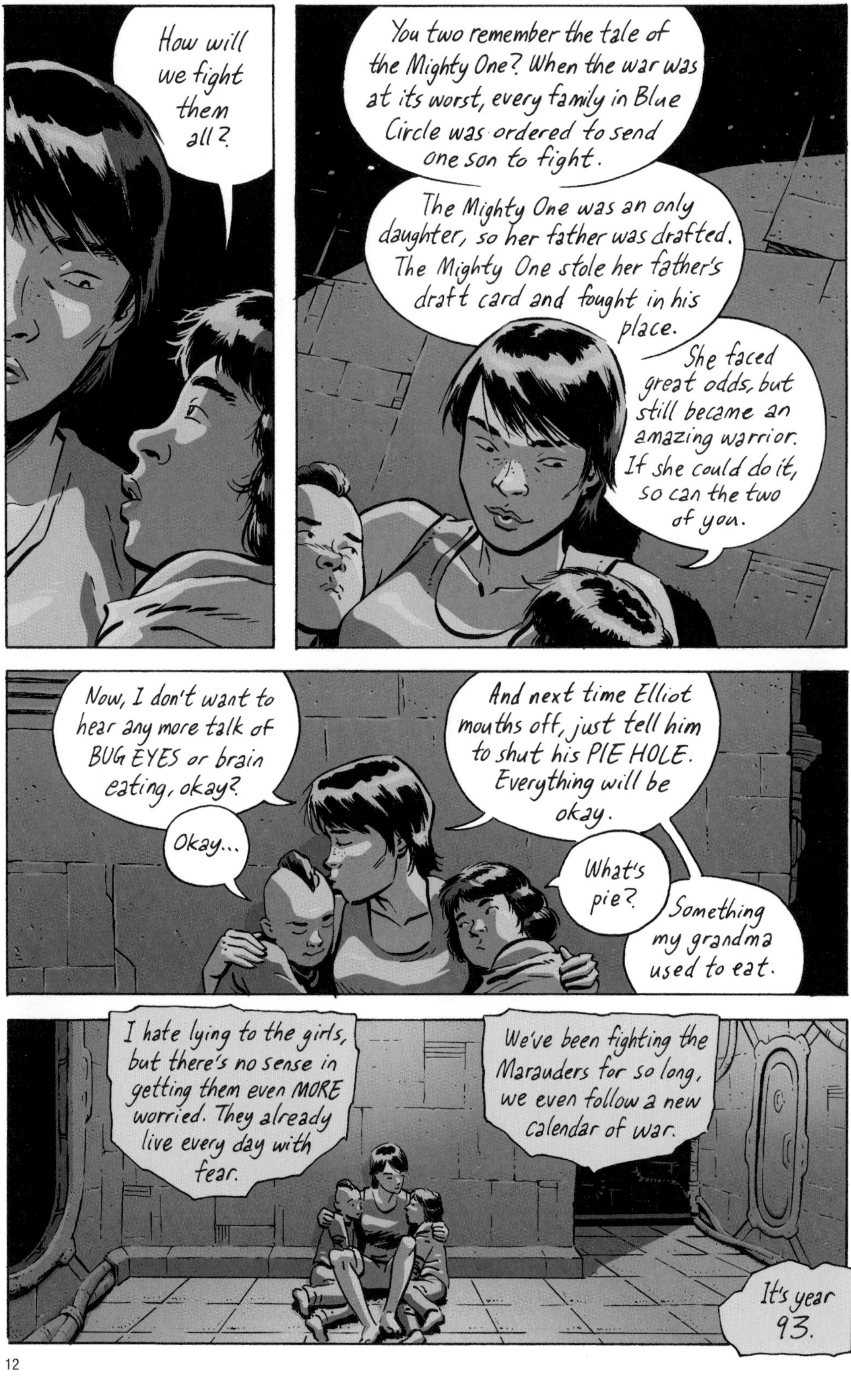

How will we fight them all?
You two remember the tale of the Mighty One? When the war was at its worst, every family in Blue Circle was ordered to send one son to fight.
The Mighty One was an only daughter, so her father was drafted. The Mighty One stole her father's draft card and fought in his place.
She faced great odds, but still became an amazing warrior. If she could do it, so can the two of you.
Now, I don't want to hear any more talk of BUG EYES or brain eating, okay?
Okay...
And next time Elliot mouths off, just tell him to shut his PIE HOLE. Everything will be okay.
What's pie?
Something my grandma used to eat.
I hate lying to the girls, but there's no sense in getting them even MORE worried. They already live every day with fear.
We've been fighting the Marauders for so long, we even follow a new calendar of war.
It's year 93.

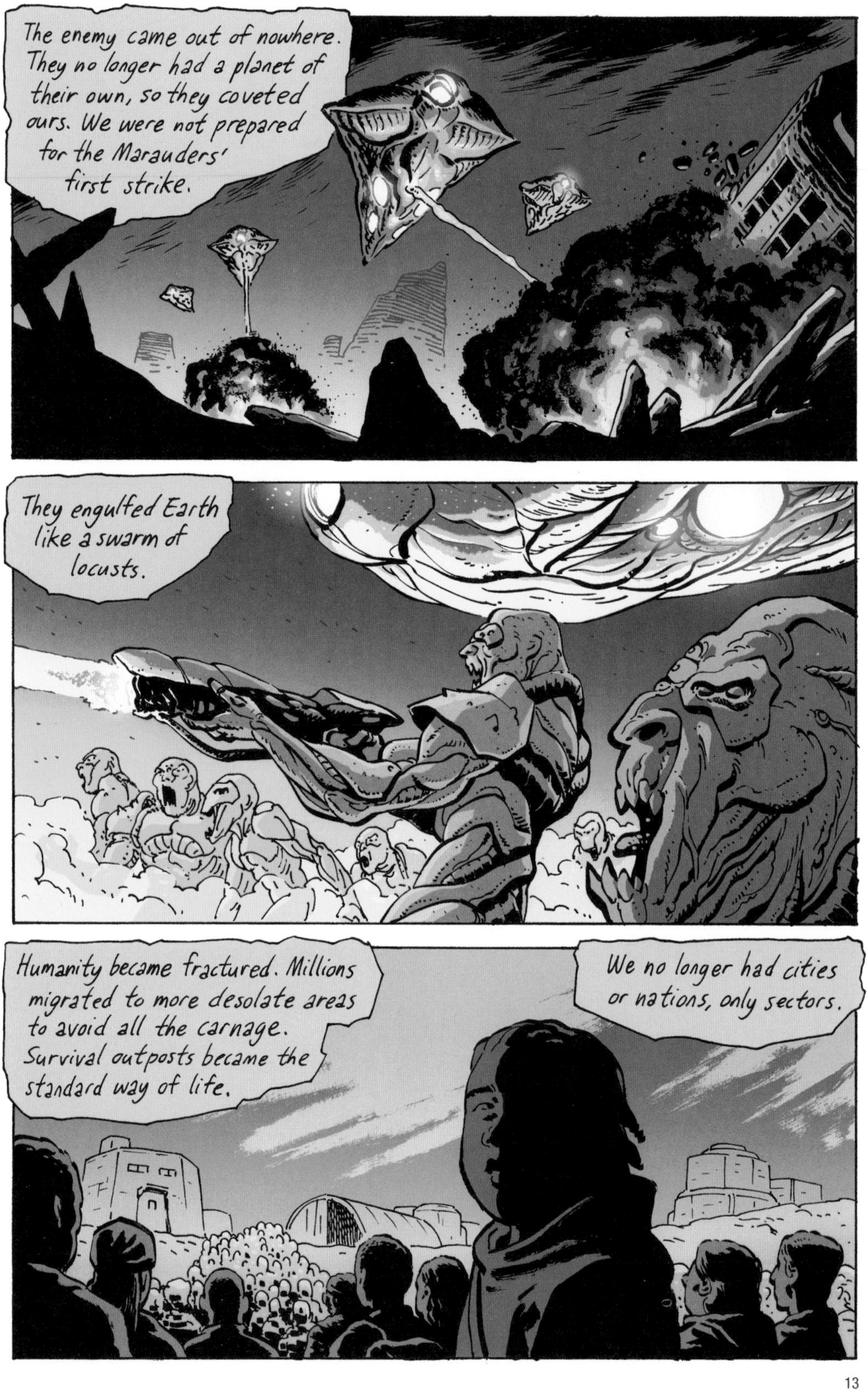
The enemy came out of nowhere. They no longer had a planet of their own, so they coveted ours. We were not prepared for the Marauders' first strike.
They engulfed Earth like a swarm of locusts.
Humanity became fractured. Millions migrated to more desolate areas to avoid all the carnage. Survival outposts became the standard way of life.
We no longer had cities or nations, only sectors.

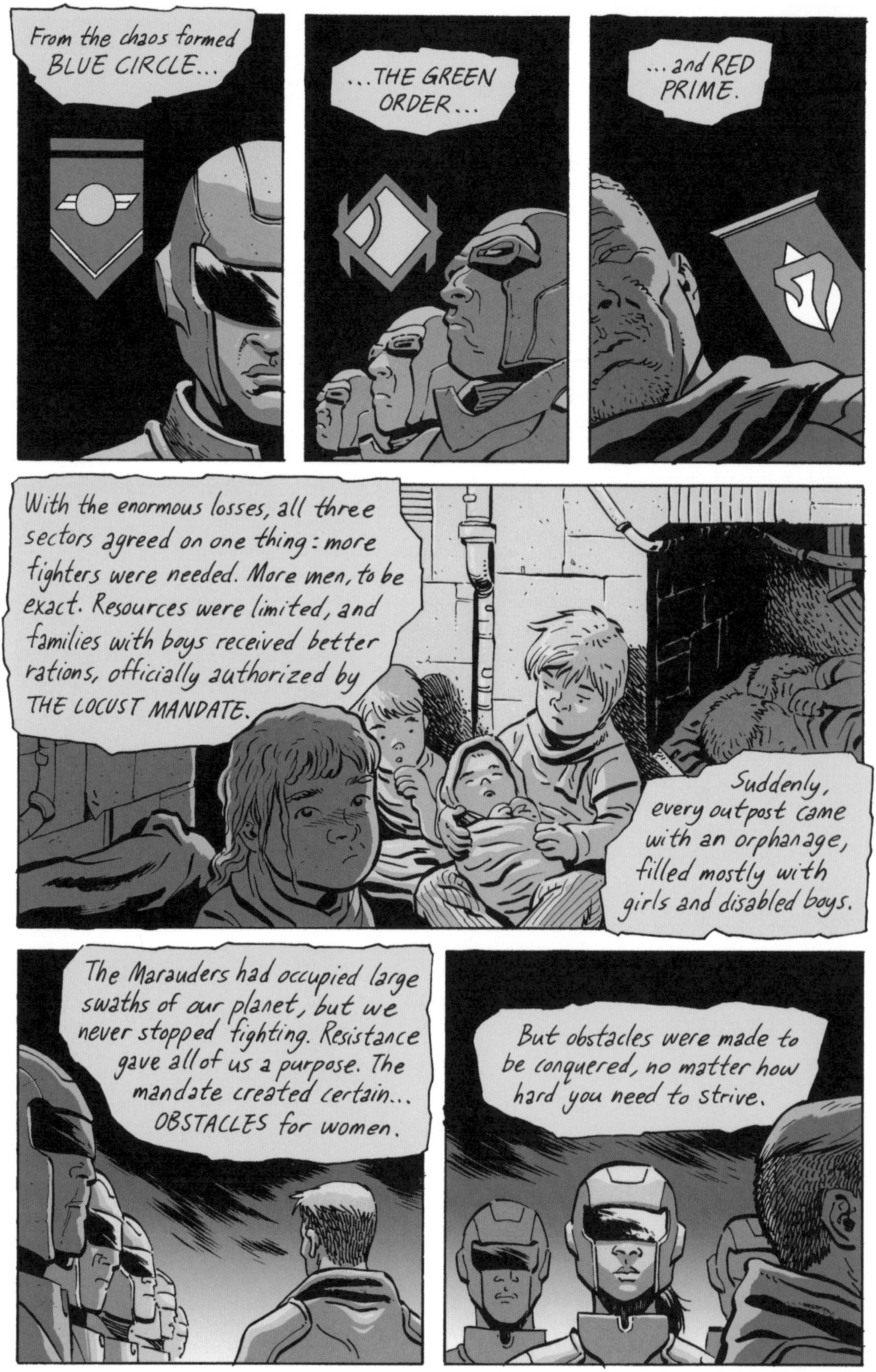
From the chaos formed BLUE CIRCLE...
...THE GREEN ORDER...
...and RED PRIME.
With the enormous losses, all three sectors agreed on one thing: more fighters were needed. More men, to be exact. Resources were limited, and families with boys received better rations, officially authorized by THE LOCUST MANDATE.
Suddenly, every outpost came with an orphanage, filled mostly with girls and disabled boys.
The Marauders had occupied large swaths of our planet, but we never stopped fighting. Resistance gave all of us a purpose. The mandate created certain... OBSTACLES for women.
But obstacles were made to be conquered, no matter how hard you need to strive.

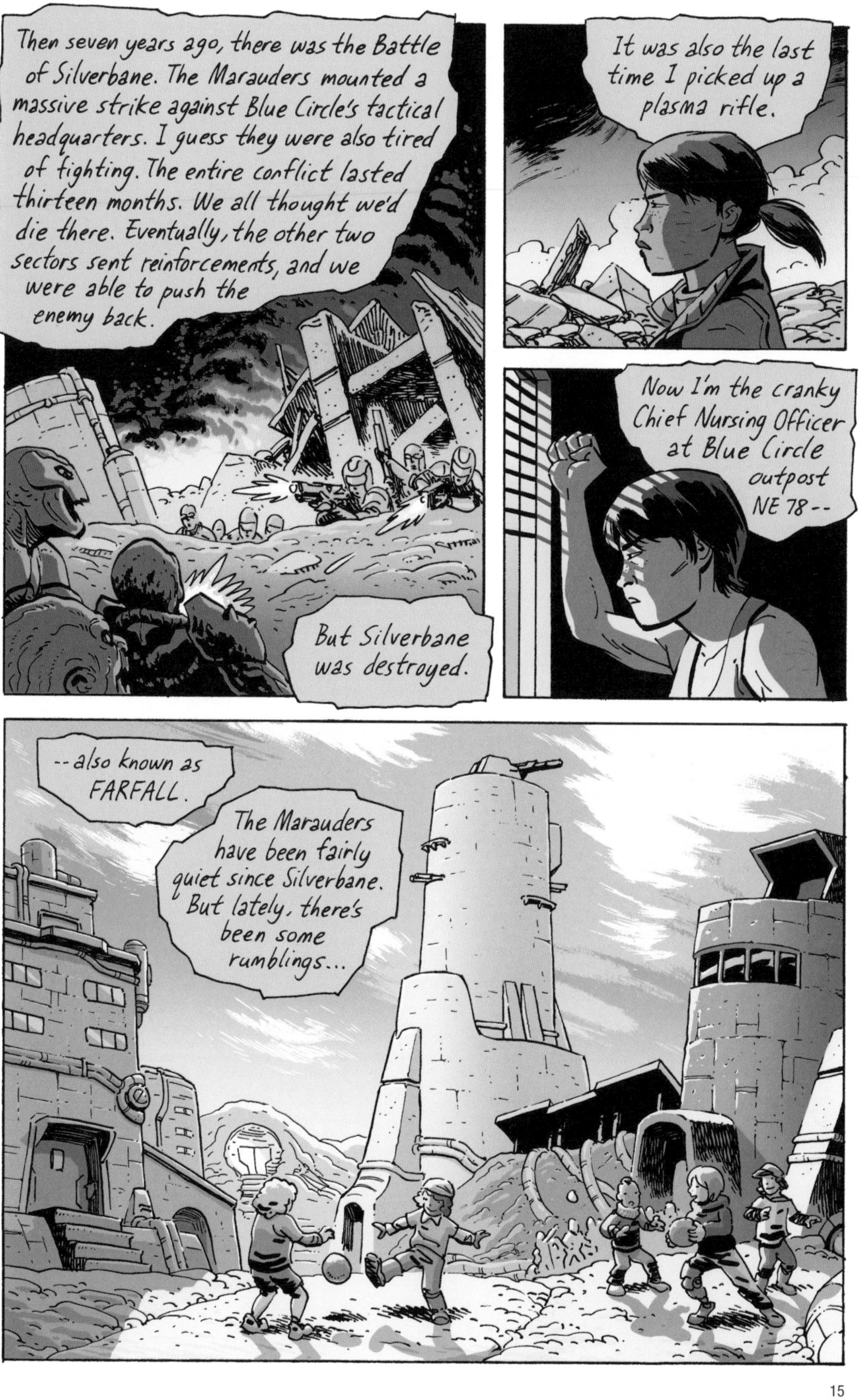

Then seven years ago, there was the Battle of Silverbane. The Marauders mounted a massive strike against Blue Circle's tactical headquarters. I guess they were also tired of fighting. The entire conflict lasted thirteen months. We all thought we'd die there. Eventually, the other two sectors sent reinforcements, and we were able to push the enemy back.
But Silverbane was destroyed.
It was also the last time I picked up a plasma rifle.
Now I'm the cranky Chief Nursing Officer at Blue Circle outpost NE 78--
--also known as FARFALL.
The Marauders have been fairly quiet since Silverbane. But lately, there's been some rumblings...

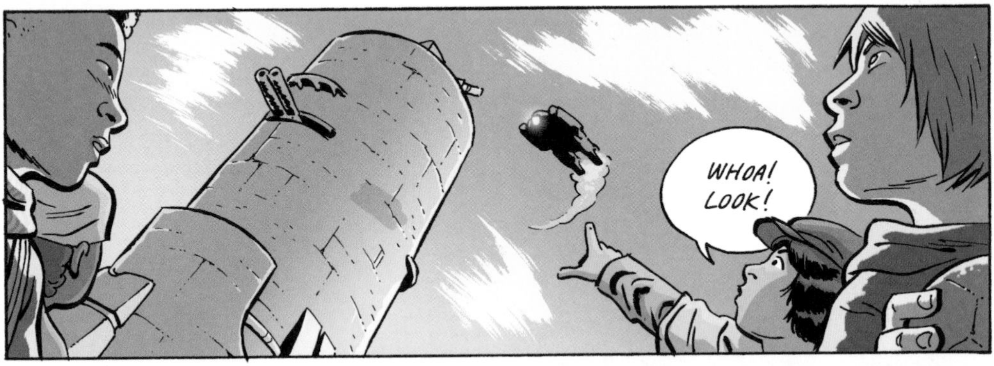
WHOA! LOOK!

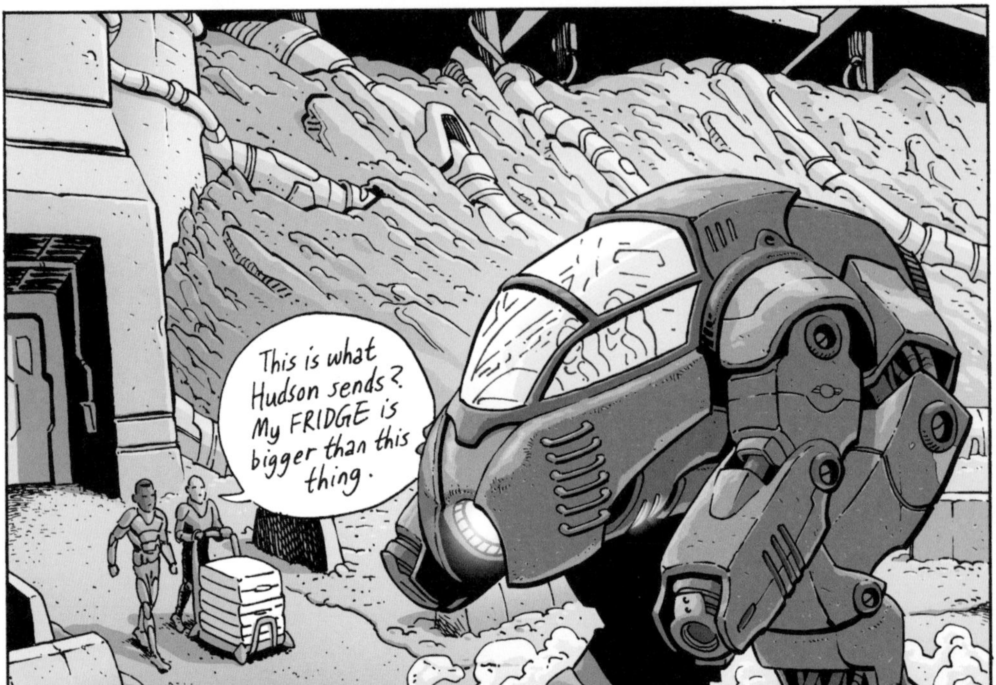
This is what Hudson sends? My FRIDGE is bigger than this thing.

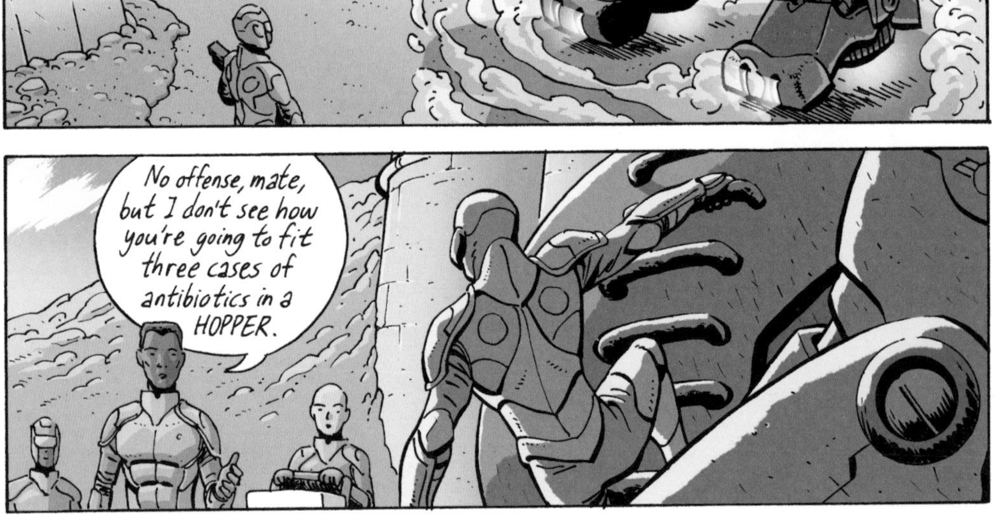
No offense, mate, but I don't see how you're going to fit three cases of antibiotics in a HOPPER.

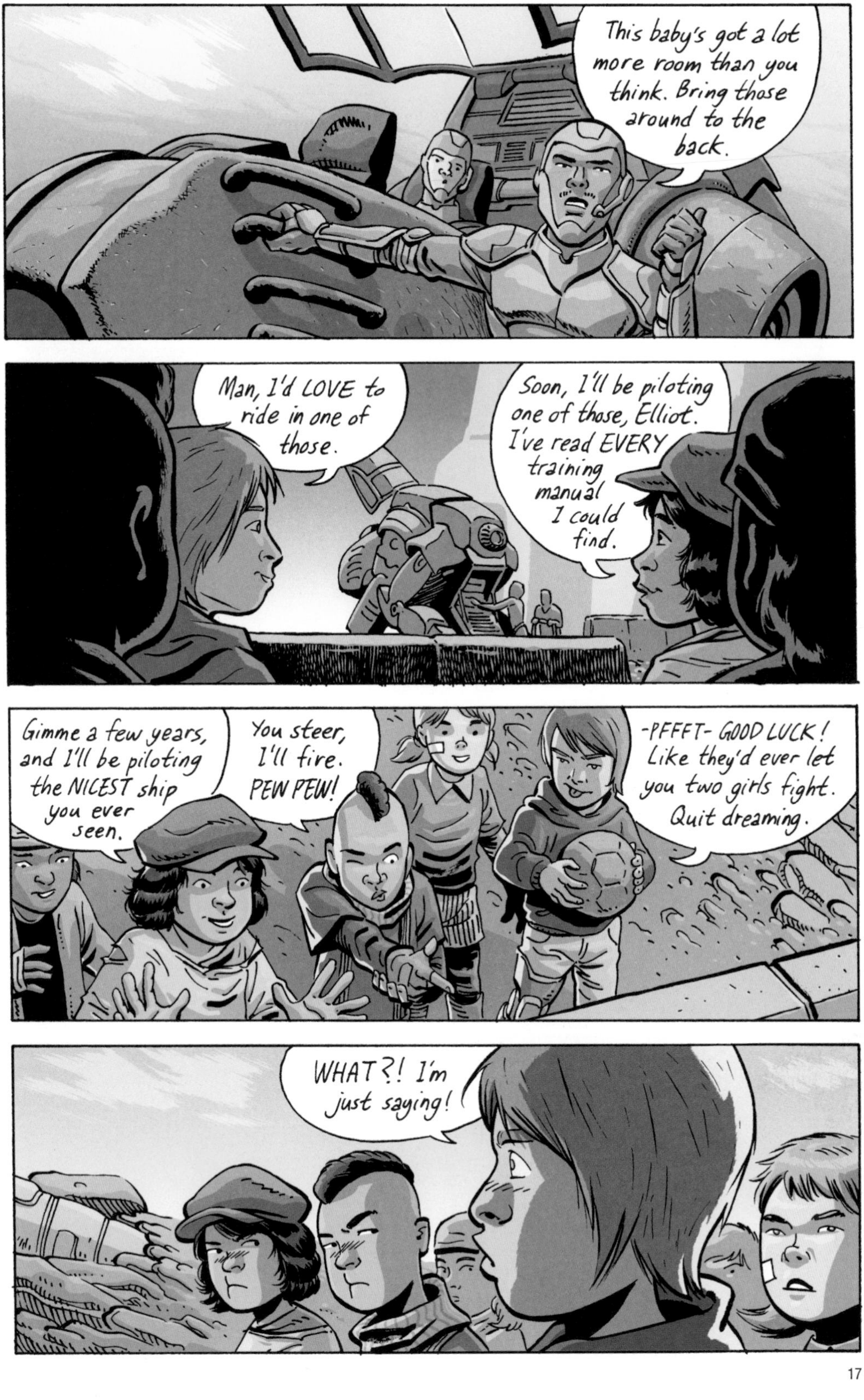
This baby's got a lot more room than you think. Bring those around to the back.
Man, I'd LOVE to ride in one of those.
Soon, I'll be piloting one of those, Elliot. I've read EVERY training manual I could find.
Gimme a few years, and I'll be piloting the NICEST ship you ever seen.
You steer, I'll fire. PEW PEW!
-PFFFT- GOOD LUCK! Like they'd ever let you two girls fight. Quit dreaming.
WHAT?! I'm just saying!

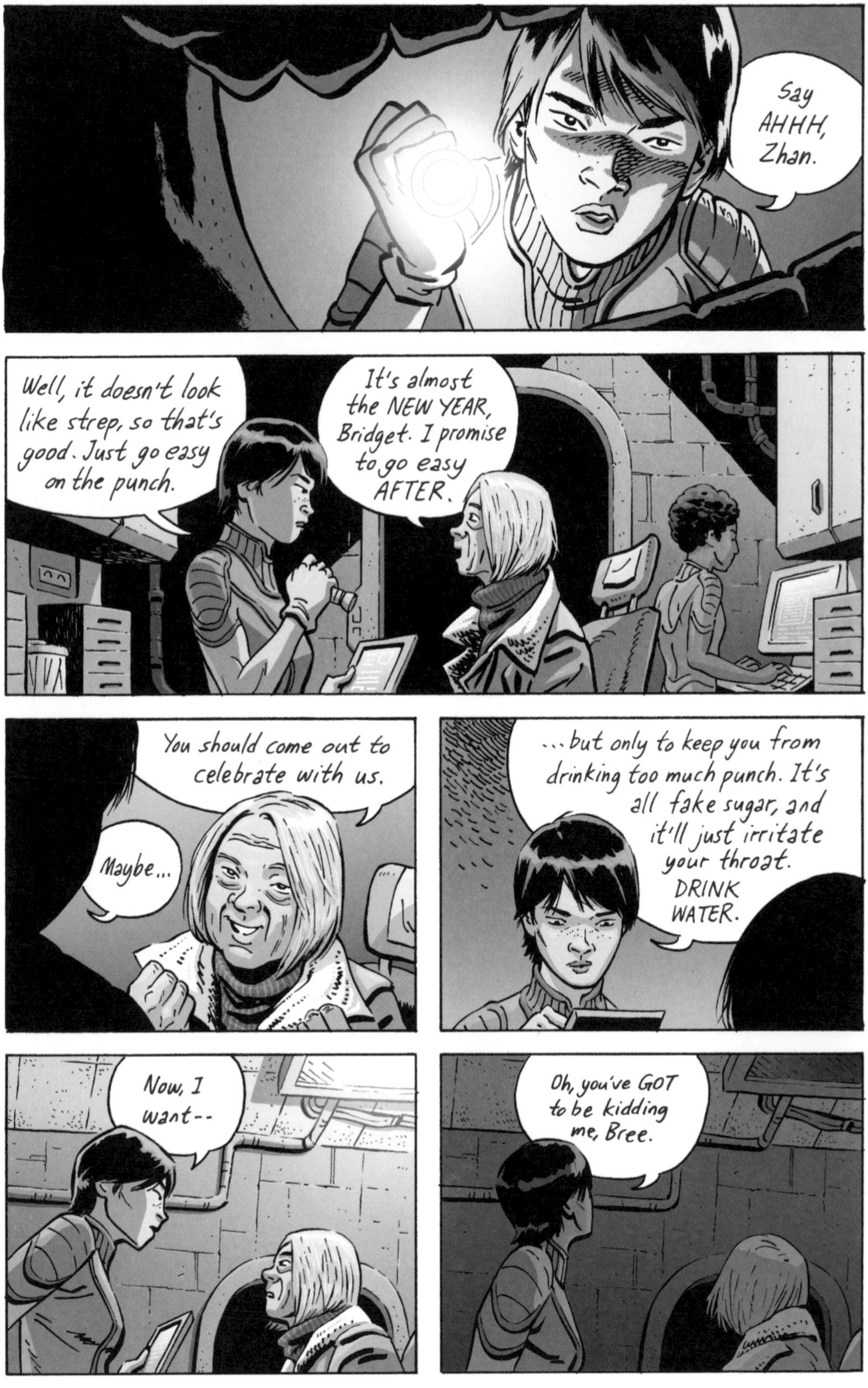
Say AHHH, Zhan.
Well, it doesn't look like strep, so that's good. Just go easy on the punch.
It's almost the NEW YEAR, Bridget. I promise to go easy AFTER.
You should come out to celebrate with us.
Maybe...
...but only to keep you from drinking too much punch. It's all fake sugar, and it'll just irritate your throat. DRINK WATER.
Now, I want--
Oh, you've GOT to be kidding me, Bree.

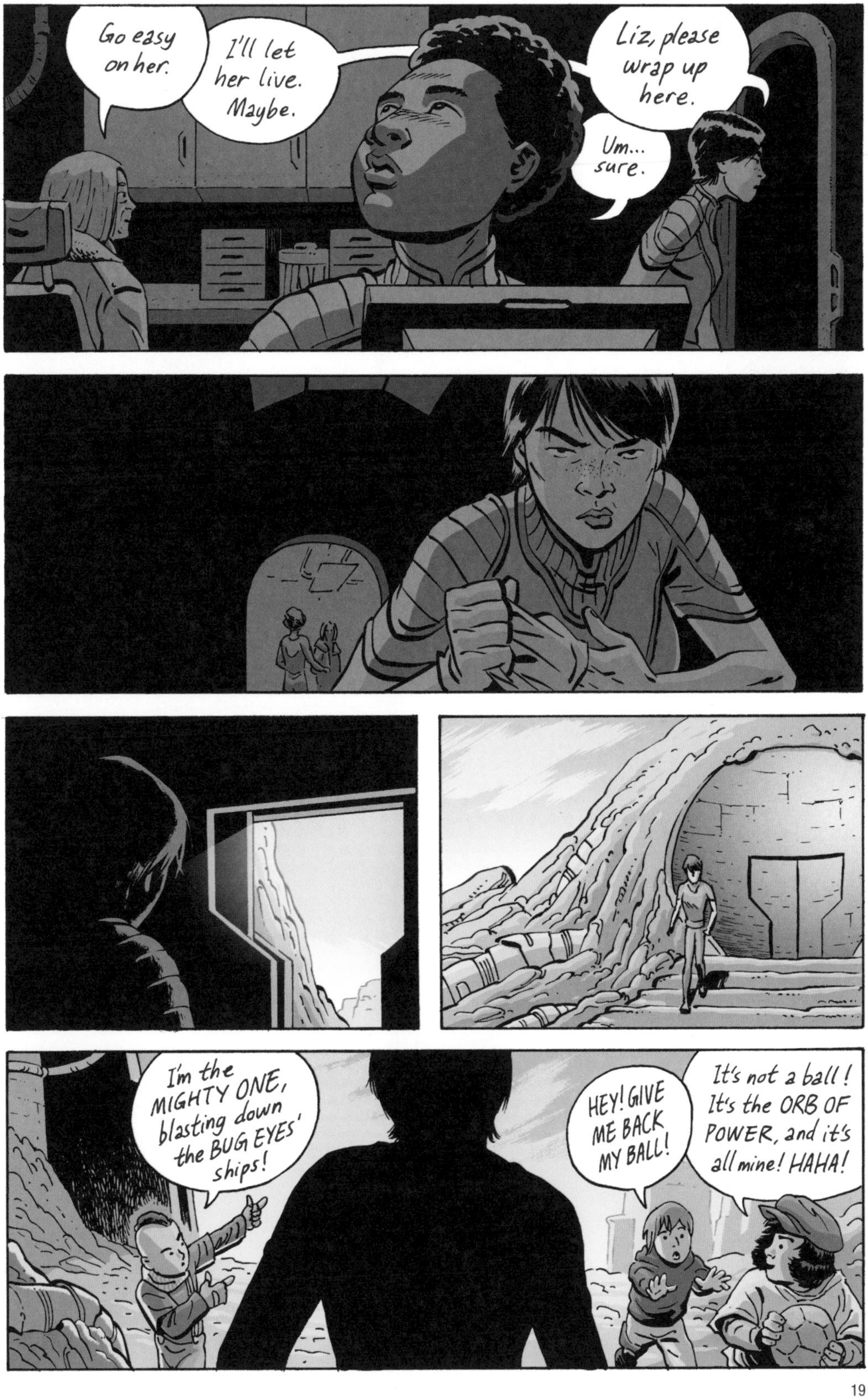
Go easy on her.
I'll let her live. Maybe.
Liz, please wrap up here.
Um... sure.
I'm the MIGHTY ONE, blasting down the BUG EYES' ships!
HEY! GIVE ME BACK MY BALL!
It's not a ball! It's the ORB OF POWER, and it's all mine! HAHA!

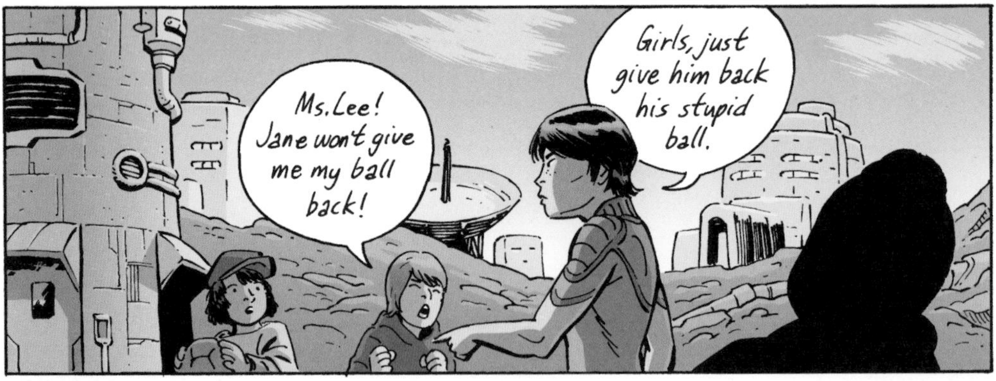
Ms.Lee! Jane won't give me my ball back!
Girls, just give him back his stupid ball.

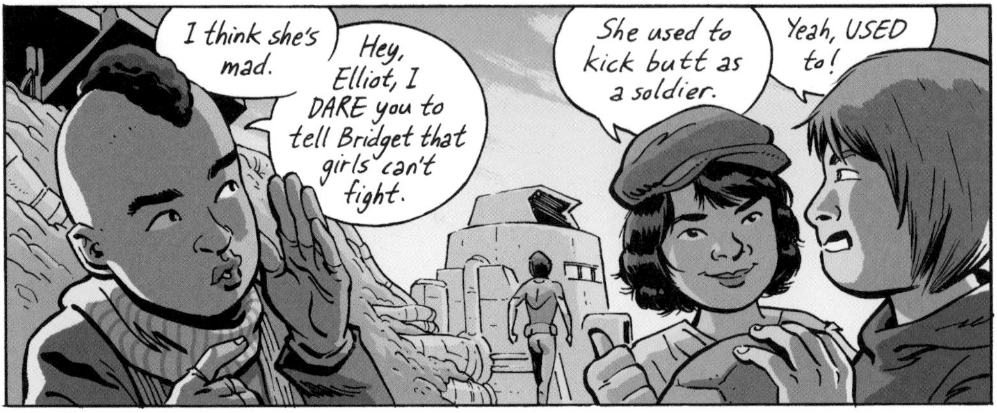
I think she's mad.
Hey, Elliot, I DARE you to tell Bridget that girls can't fight.
She used to kick butt as a soldier.
Yeah, USED to!

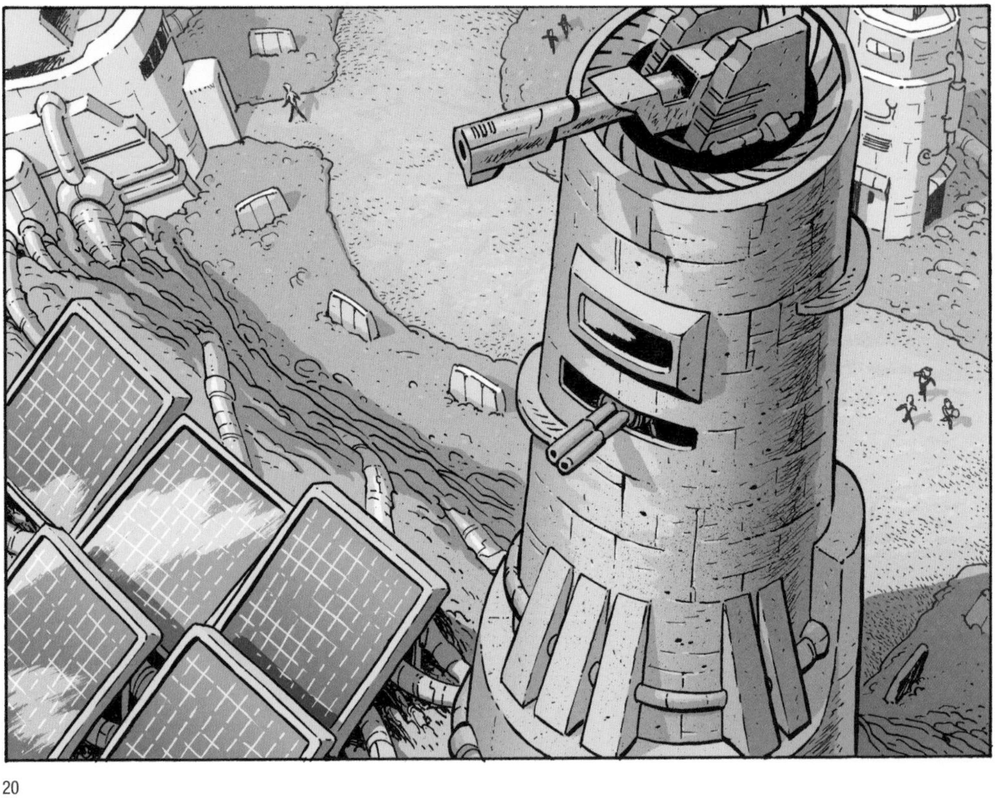

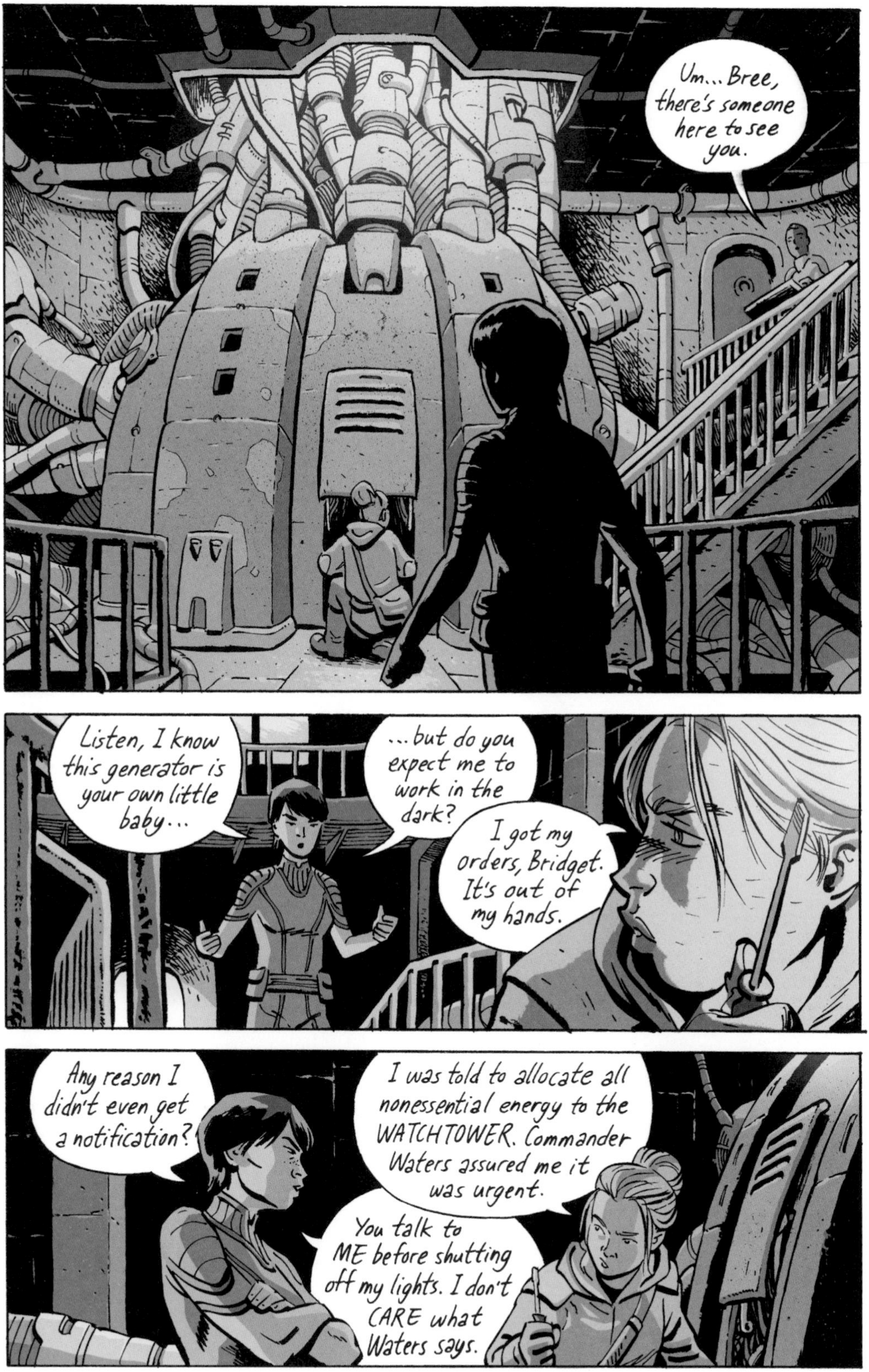
Um... Bree, there's someone here to see you.
Listen, I know this generator is your own little baby...
...but do you expect me to work in the dark?
I got my orders, Bridget. It's out of my hands.
Any reason I didn't even get a notification?
I was told to allocate all nonessential energy to the WATCHTOWER. Commander Waters assured me it was urgent.
You talk to ME before shutting off my lights. I don't CARE what Waters says.

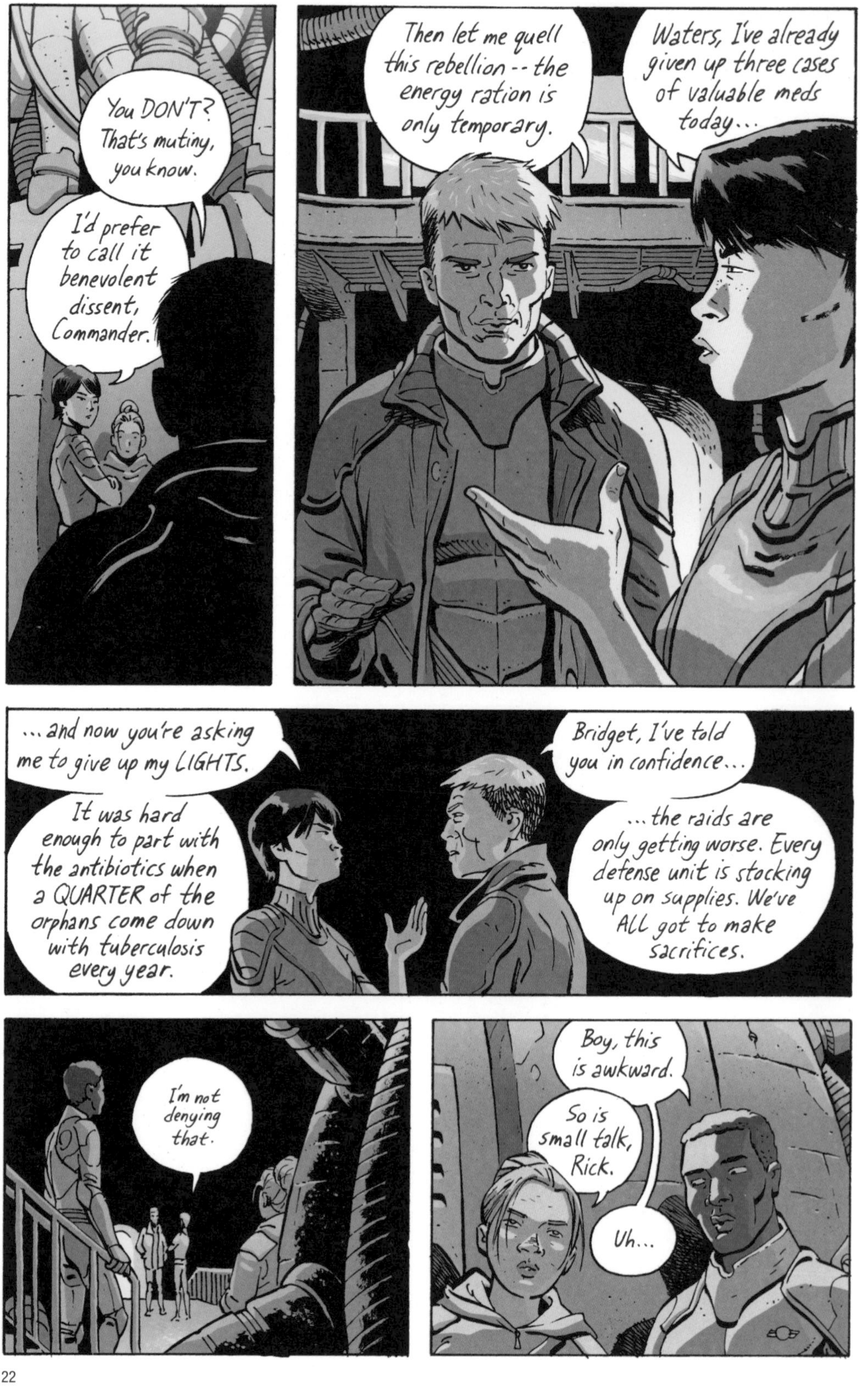
You DON'T? That's mutiny, you know.
I'd prefer to call it benevolent dissent, Commander.
Then let me quell this rebellion -- the energy ration is only temporary.
Waters, I've already given up three cases of valuable meds today...
...and now you're asking me to give up my LIGHTS.
It was hard enough to part with the antibiotics when a QUARTER of the orphans come down with tuberculosis every year.
Bridget, I've told you in confidence...
...the raids are only getting worse. Every defense unit is stocking up on supplies. We've ALL got to make sacrifices.
I'm not denying that.
Boy, this is awkward.
So is small talk, Rick.
Uh...

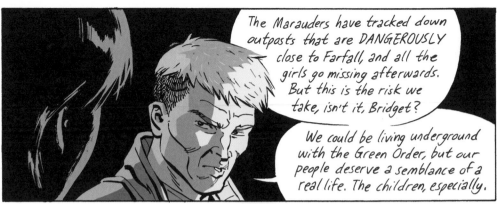

The Marauders have tracked down outposts that are DANGEROUSLY close to Farfall, and all the girls go missing afterwards. But this is the risk we take, isn't it, Bridget?

We could be living underground with the Green Order, but our people deserve a semblance of a real life. The children, especially.

Every commander has been given the same order: keep the watchtower ready. You need lights. I NEED LASER CANNONS.

Waters, don't use the CHILDREN to make your argument. We both know that the orphans are just collateral to Blue Circle.

I've clocked more BUG EYES than all the newbies you've trained here. We've fought side by side, Waters, so I know what's at stake. I DO.

Yeah, sure, hang around and talk. Bree doesn't have any work to do...

I'm not here to patronize you...

...but even James would've agreed with me.

Yeah, well...

...he wasn't always the brightest.

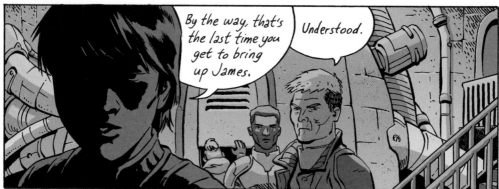

By the way, that's the last time you get to bring up James.

Understood.

I forgot that Ms. Lee used to fight in the war. She was just a medic, though, wasn't she?

Rick, there's no such thing as JUST a medic.

You couldn't imagine the odds we faced at Silverbane. Bridget had to be a medic, a gunner, and a brawler. And she was the best shot that I'VE ever seen, too.

Ms. Lee isn't here anymore, sir. You don't have to build her up. I'm sure she was decent.

You doubting me, newbie? Believe me, she was the best ever with a plasma rifle.

HA! Were the Marauders all standing still?

ENOUGH.

...Sorry.

IDIOT.

24

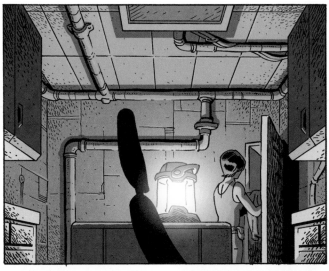

I know what awaits me when I go to sleep.

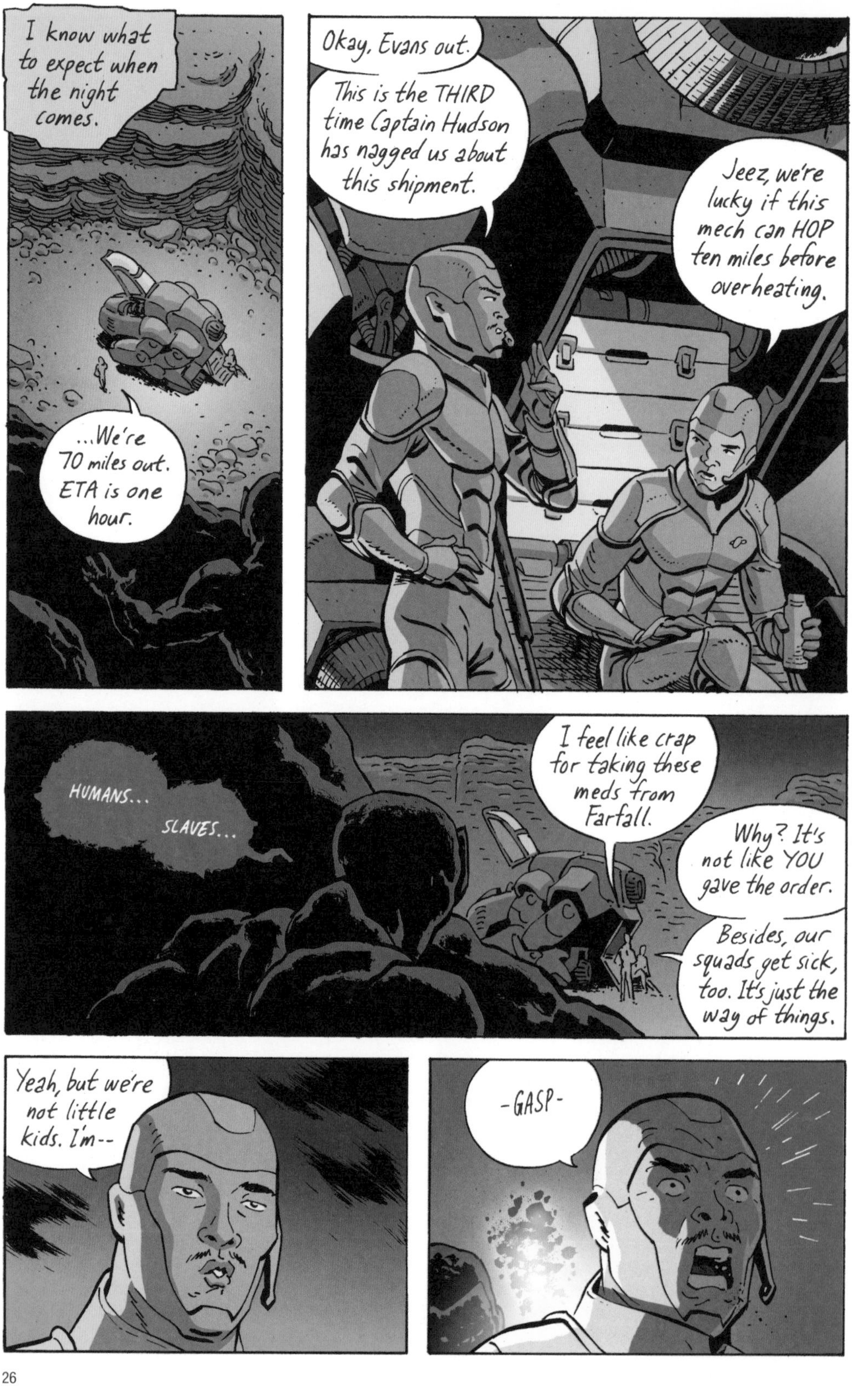
I know what to expect when the night comes.
...We're 70 miles out. ETA is one hour.
Okay, Evans out.
This is the THIRD time Captain Hudson has nagged us about this shipment.
Jeez, we're lucky if this mech can HOP ten miles before overheating.
HUMANS...
SLAVES...
I feel like crap for taking these meds from Farfall.
Why? It's not like YOU gave the order.
Besides, our squads get sick, too. It's just the way of things.
Yeah, but we're not little kids. I'm--
-GASP-

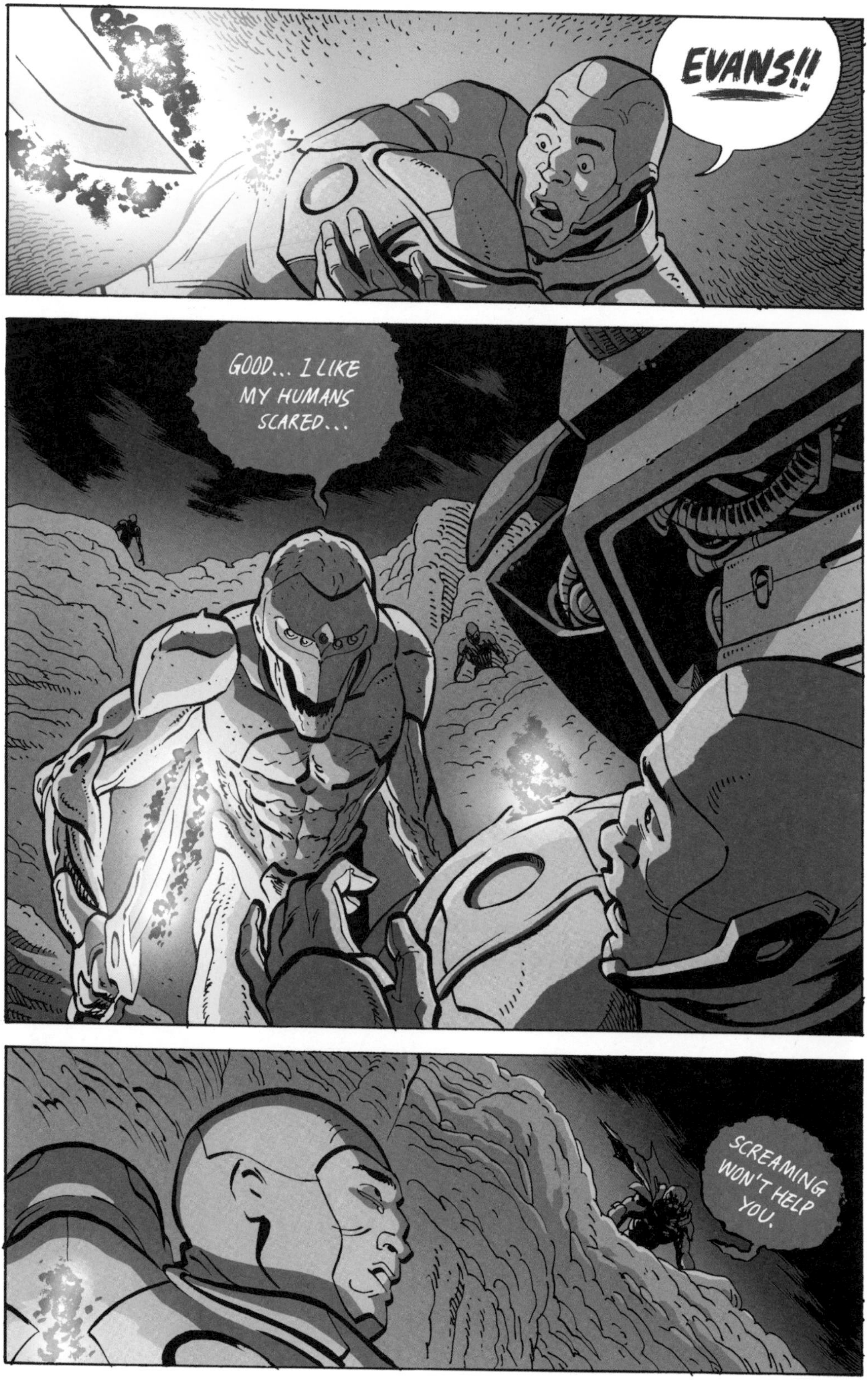

EVANS!!
GOOD... I LIKE MY HUMANS SCARED...
SCREAMING WON'T HELP YOU.

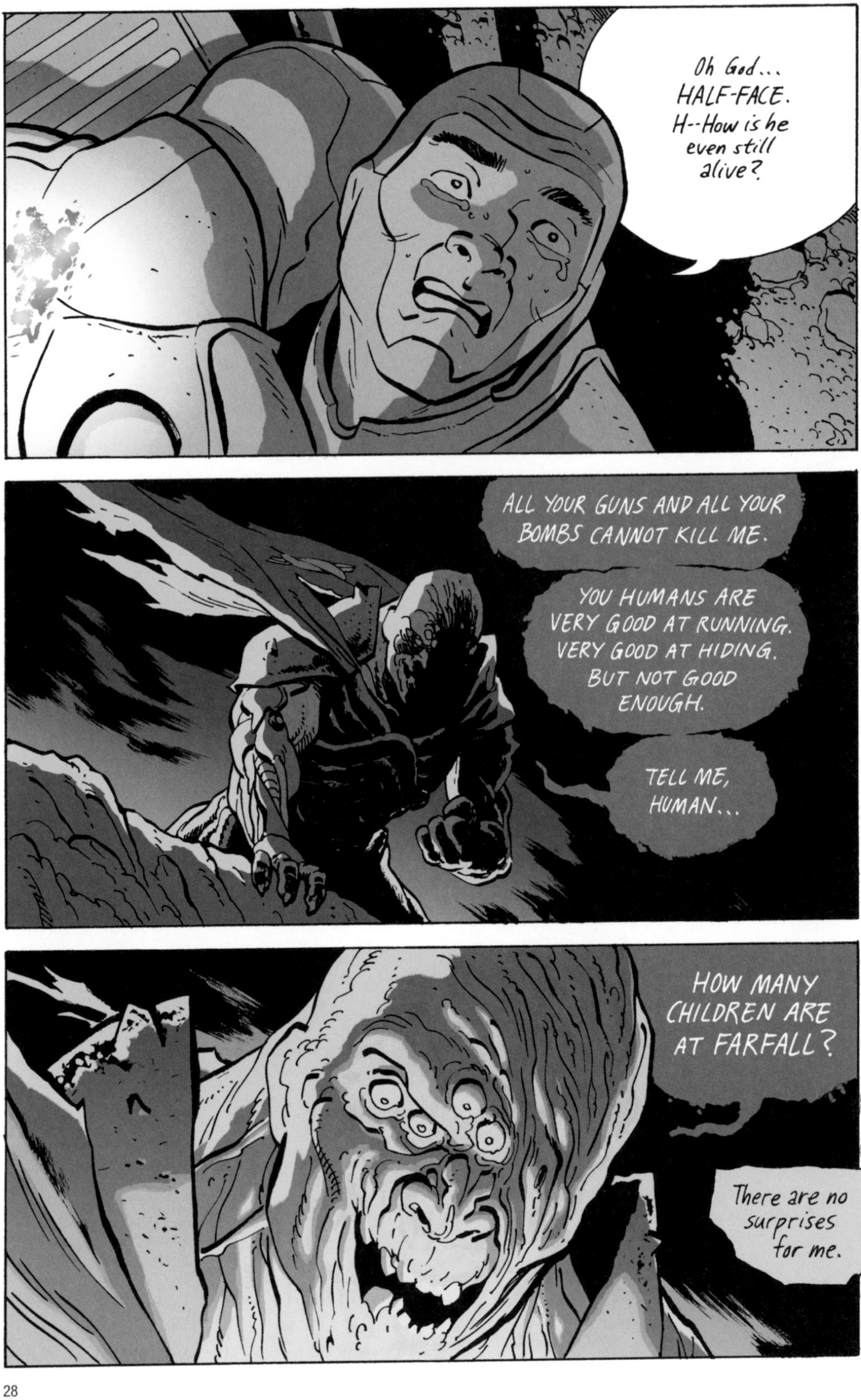
Oh God... HALF-FACE. H--How is he even still alive?
ALL YOUR GUNS AND ALL YOUR BOMBS CANNOT KILL ME.
YOU HUMANS ARE VERY GOOD AT RUNNING. VERY GOOD AT HIDING. BUT NOT GOOD ENOUGH.
TELL ME, HUMAN...
HOW MANY CHILDREN ARE AT FARFALL?
There are no surprises for me.

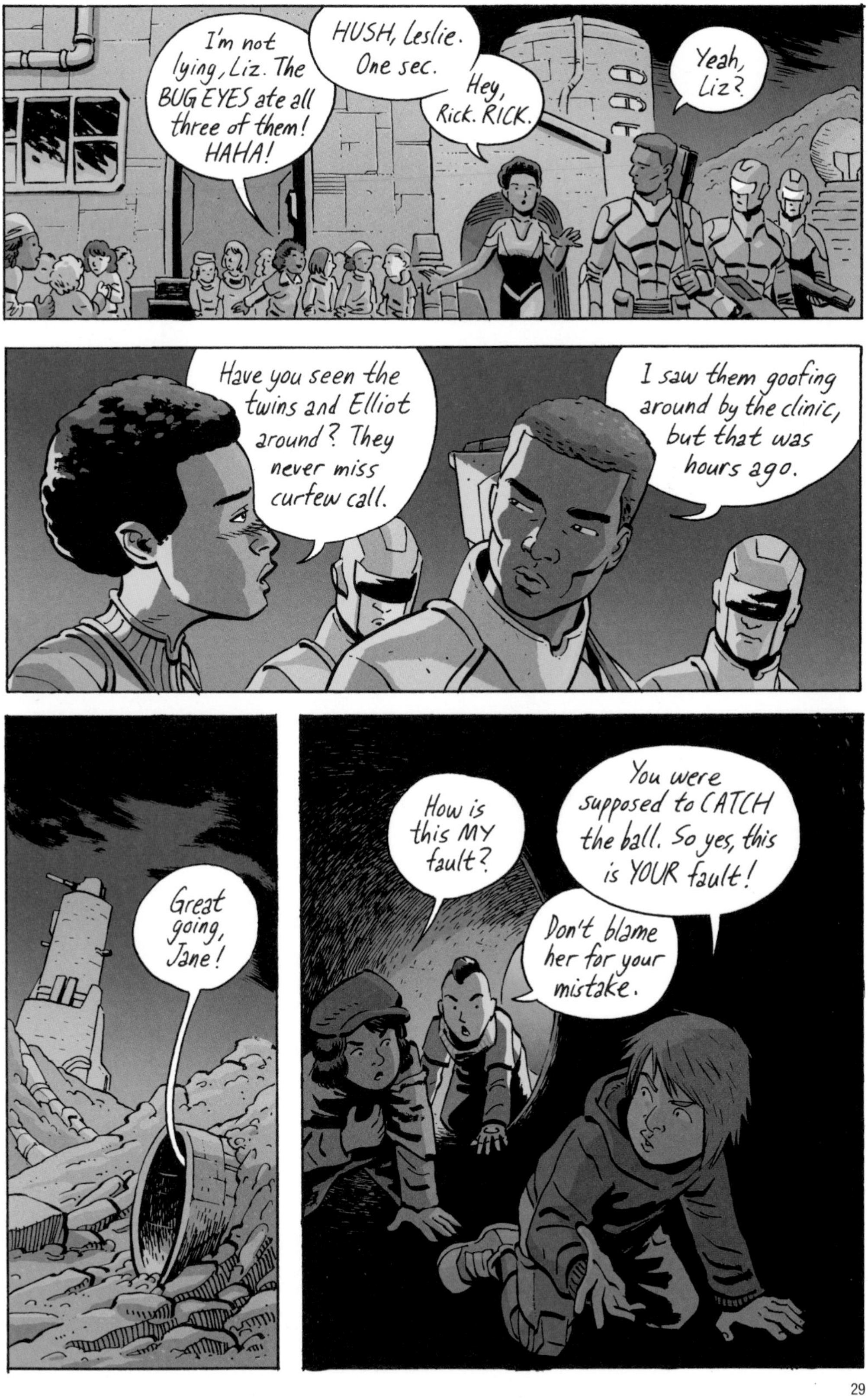
I'm not lying, Liz. The BUG EYES ate all three of them! HAHA!
HUSH, Leslie. One sec.
Hey, Rick. RICK.
Yeah, Liz?
Have you seen the twins and Elliot around? They never miss curfew call.
I saw them goofing around by the clinic, but that was hours ago.
Great going, Jane!
How is this MY fault?
You were supposed to CATCH the ball. So yes, this is YOUR fault!
Don't blame her for your mistake.

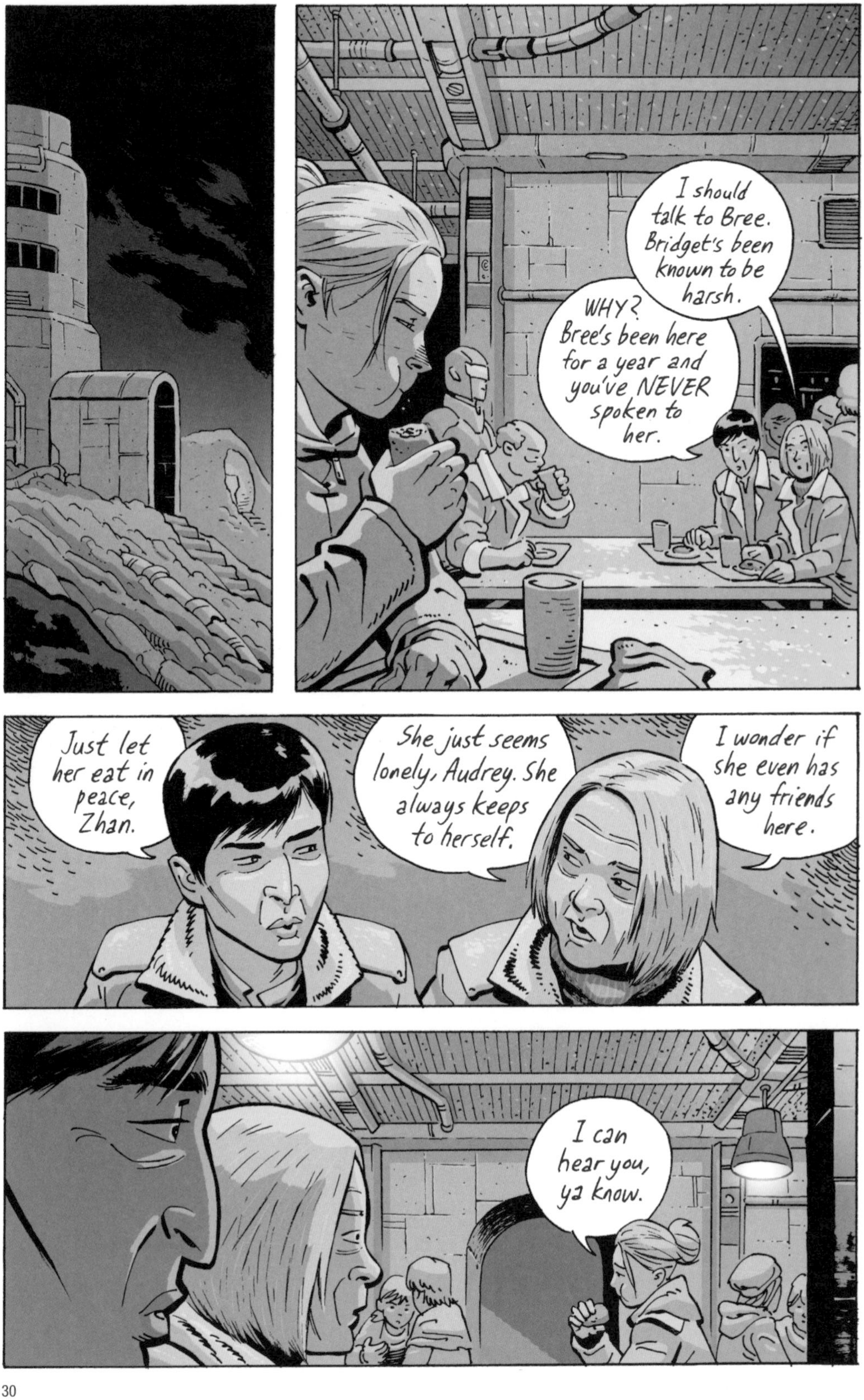
I should talk to Bree. Bridget's been known to be harsh.
WHY? Bree's been here for a year and you've NEVER spoken to her.
Just let her eat in peace, Zhan.
She just seems lonely, Audrey. She always keeps to herself.
I wonder if she even has any friends here.
I can hear you, ya know.

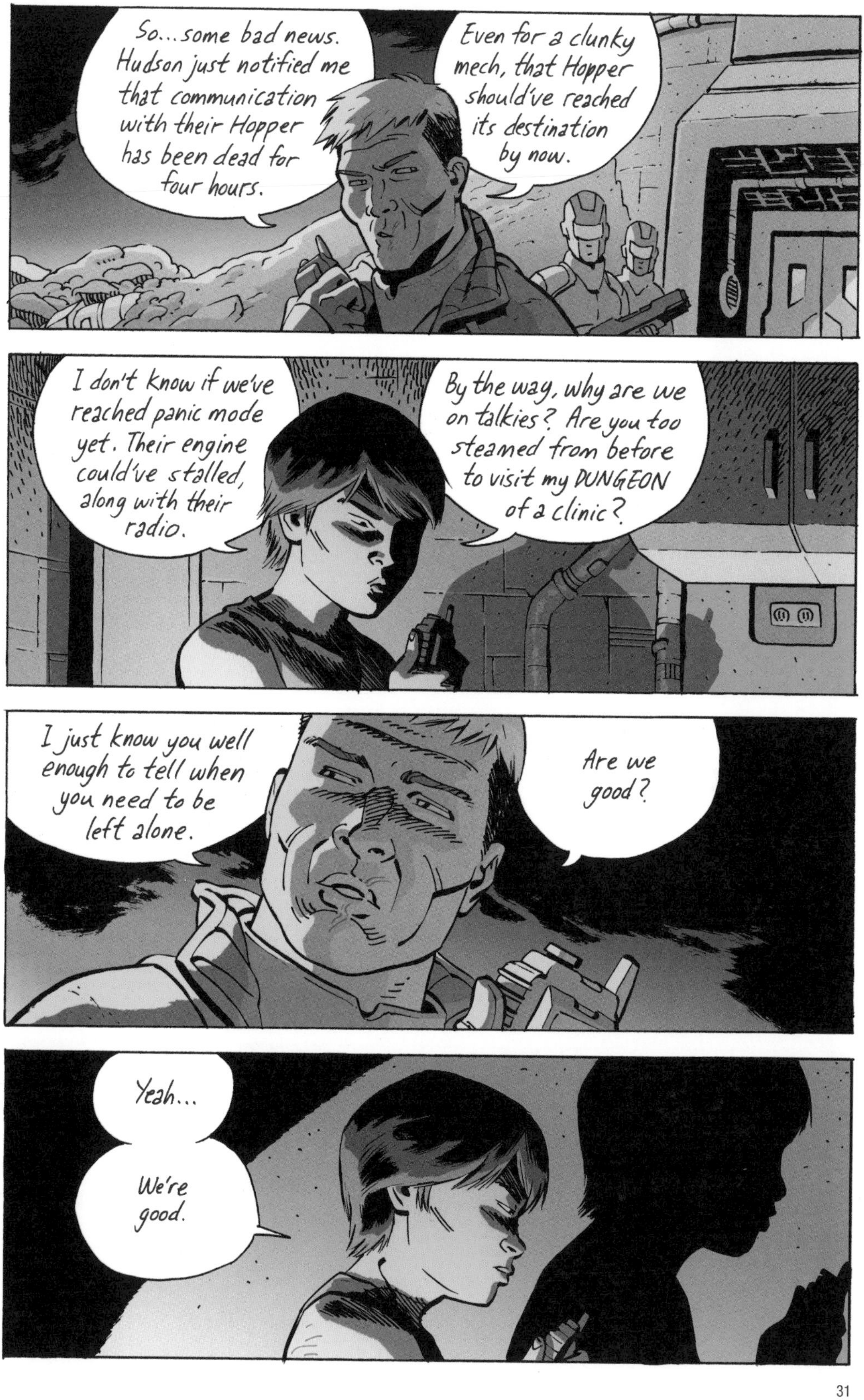
So... some bad news. Hudson just notified me that communication with their Hopper has been dead for four hours.
Even for a clunky mech, that Hopper should've reached its destination by now.
I don't know if we've reached panic mode yet. Their engine could've stalled, along with their radio.
By the way, why are we on talkies? Are you too steamed from before to visit my DUNGEON of a clinic?
I just know you well enough to tell when you need to be left alone.
Are we good?
Yeah...
We're good.

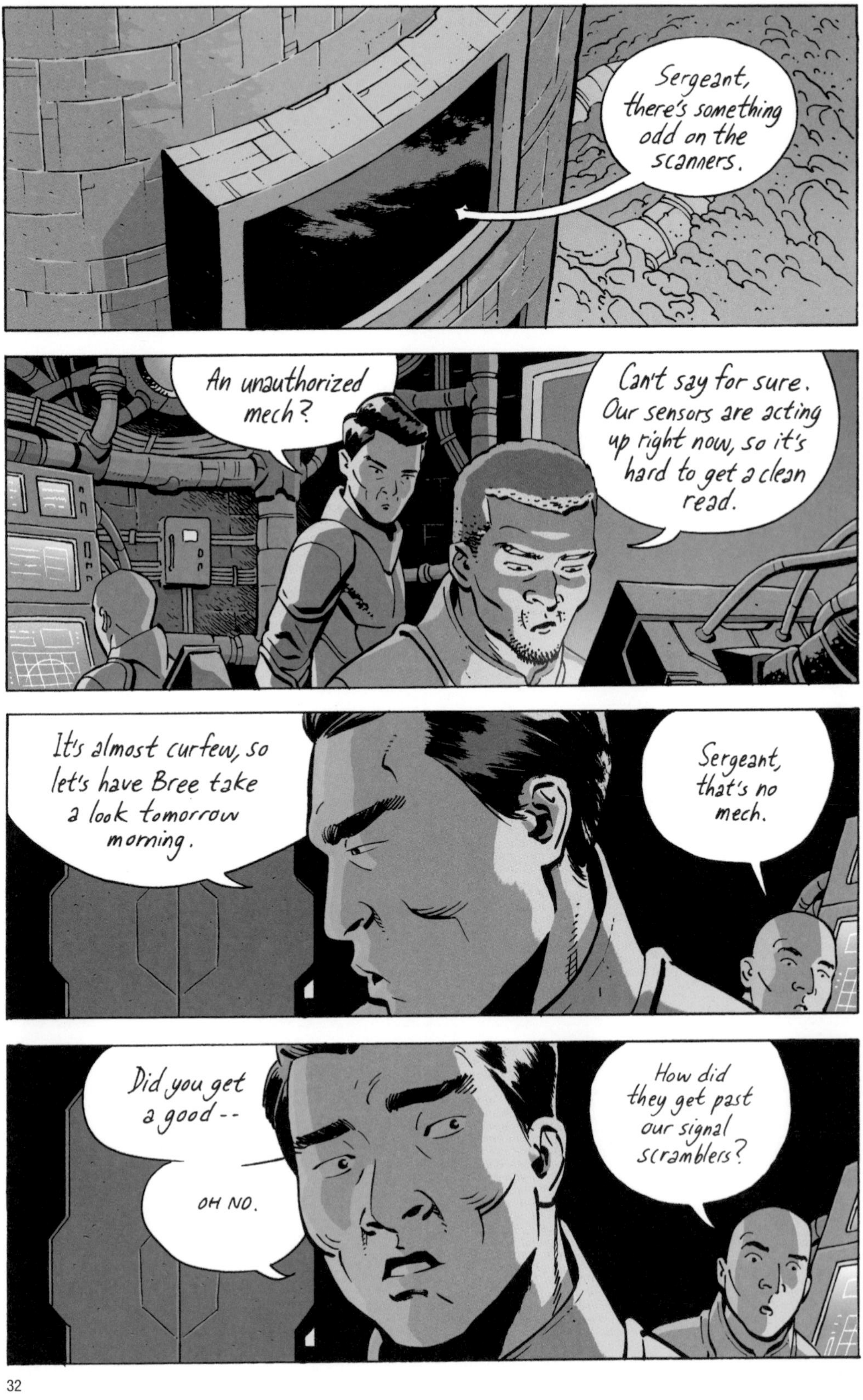
Sergeant, there's something odd on the scanners.
An unauthorized mech?
Can't say for sure. Our sensors are acting up right now, so it's hard to get a clean read.
It's almost curfew, so let's have Bree take a look tomorrow morning.
Sergeant, that's no mech.
Did you get a good --
OH NO.
How did they get past our signal scramblers?

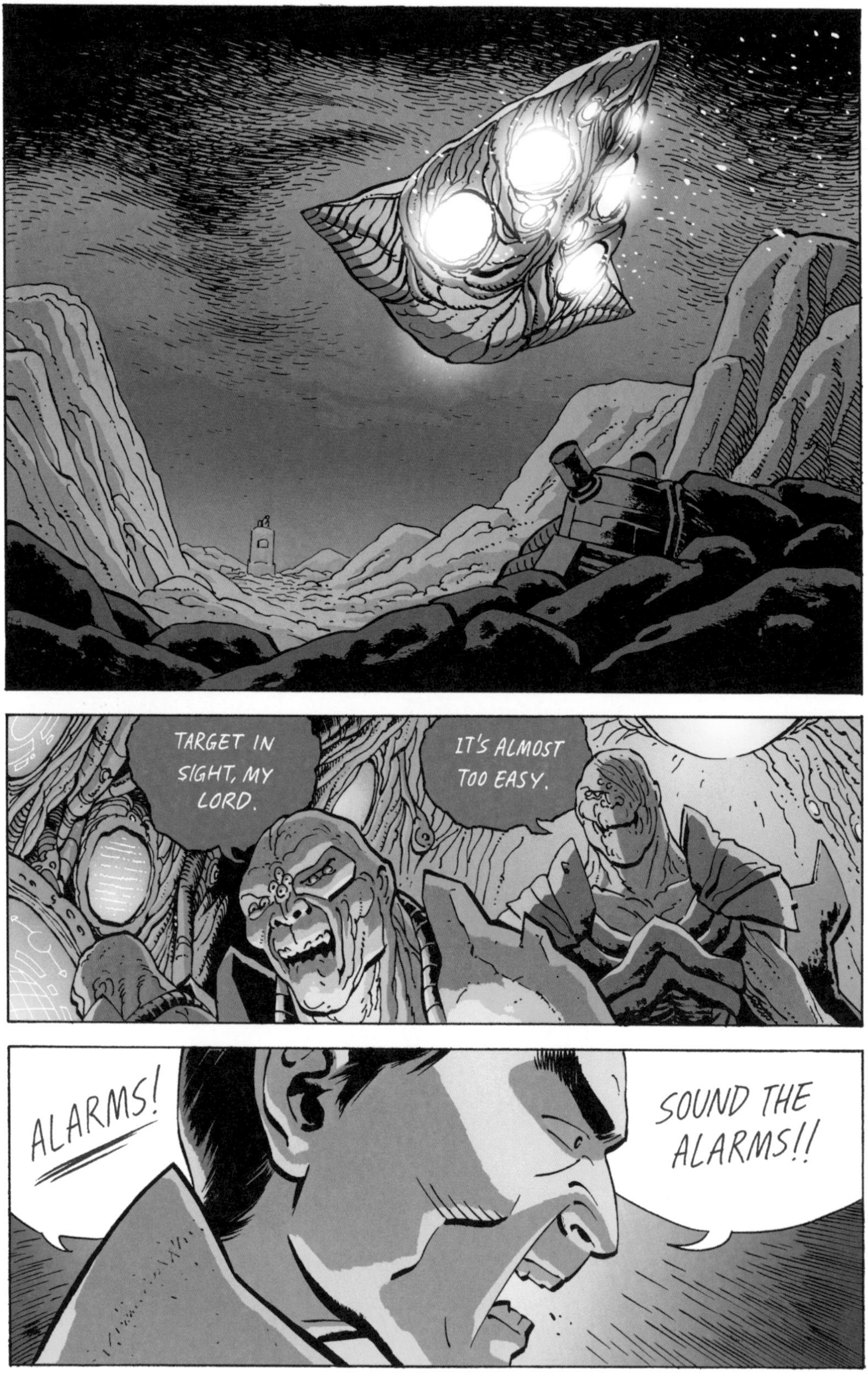
TARGET IN SIGHT, MY LORD.
IT'S ALMOST TOO EASY.
ALARMS!
SOUND THE ALARMS!!

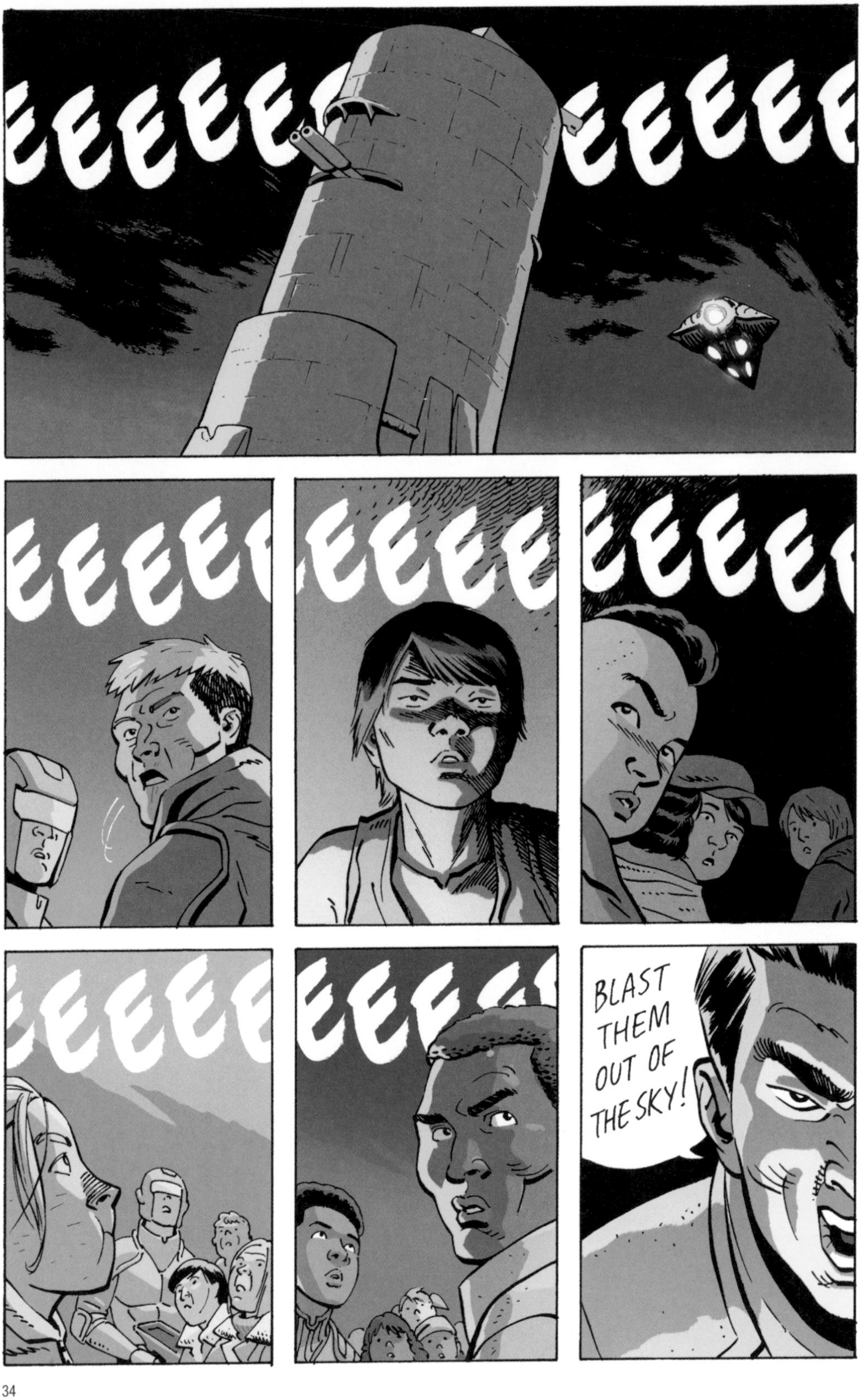
EEEEEEEEEEEE
EEEEE
EEEEEE
EEEEE
EEEEE
EEEE
BLAST THEM OUT OF THE SKY!

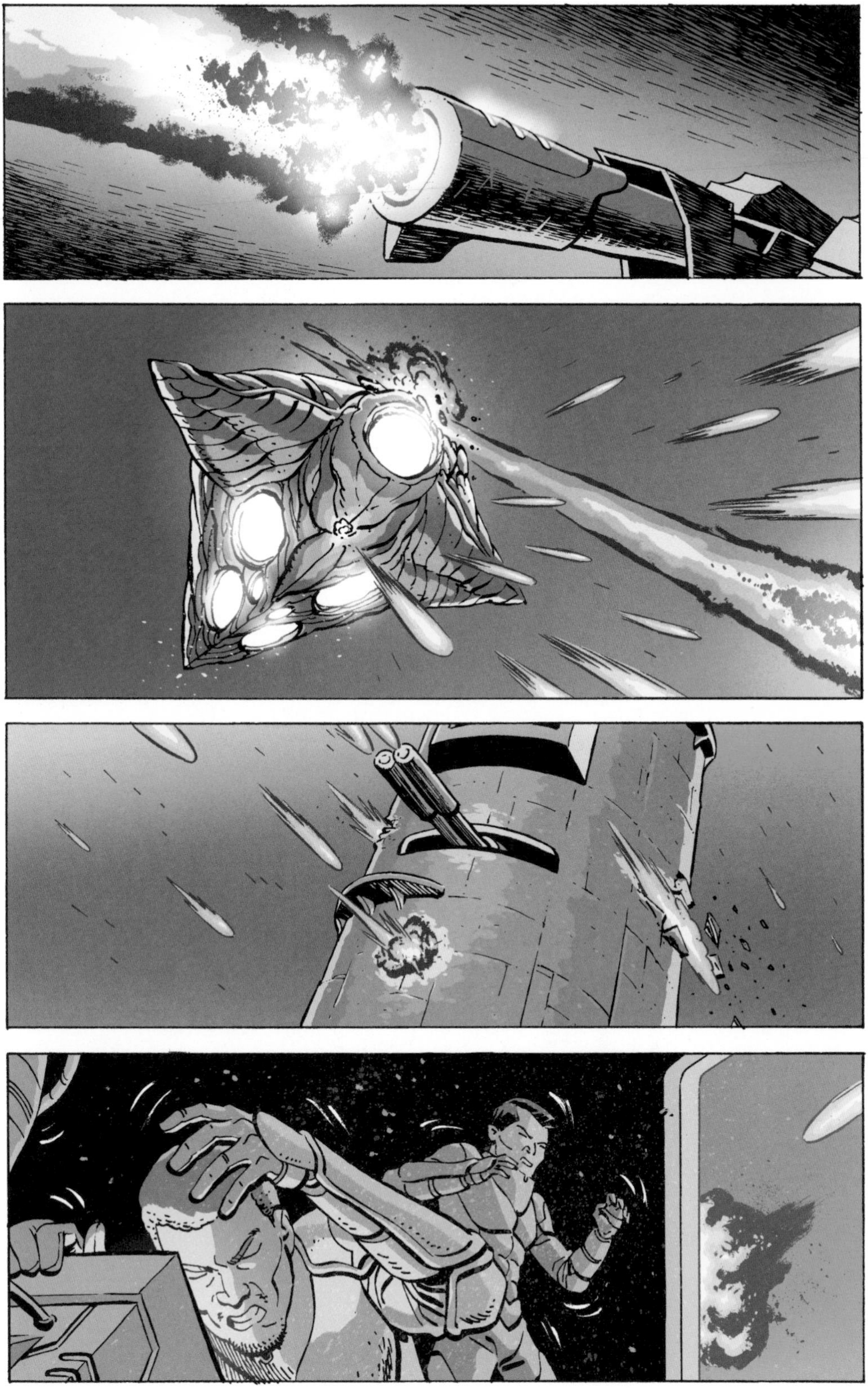

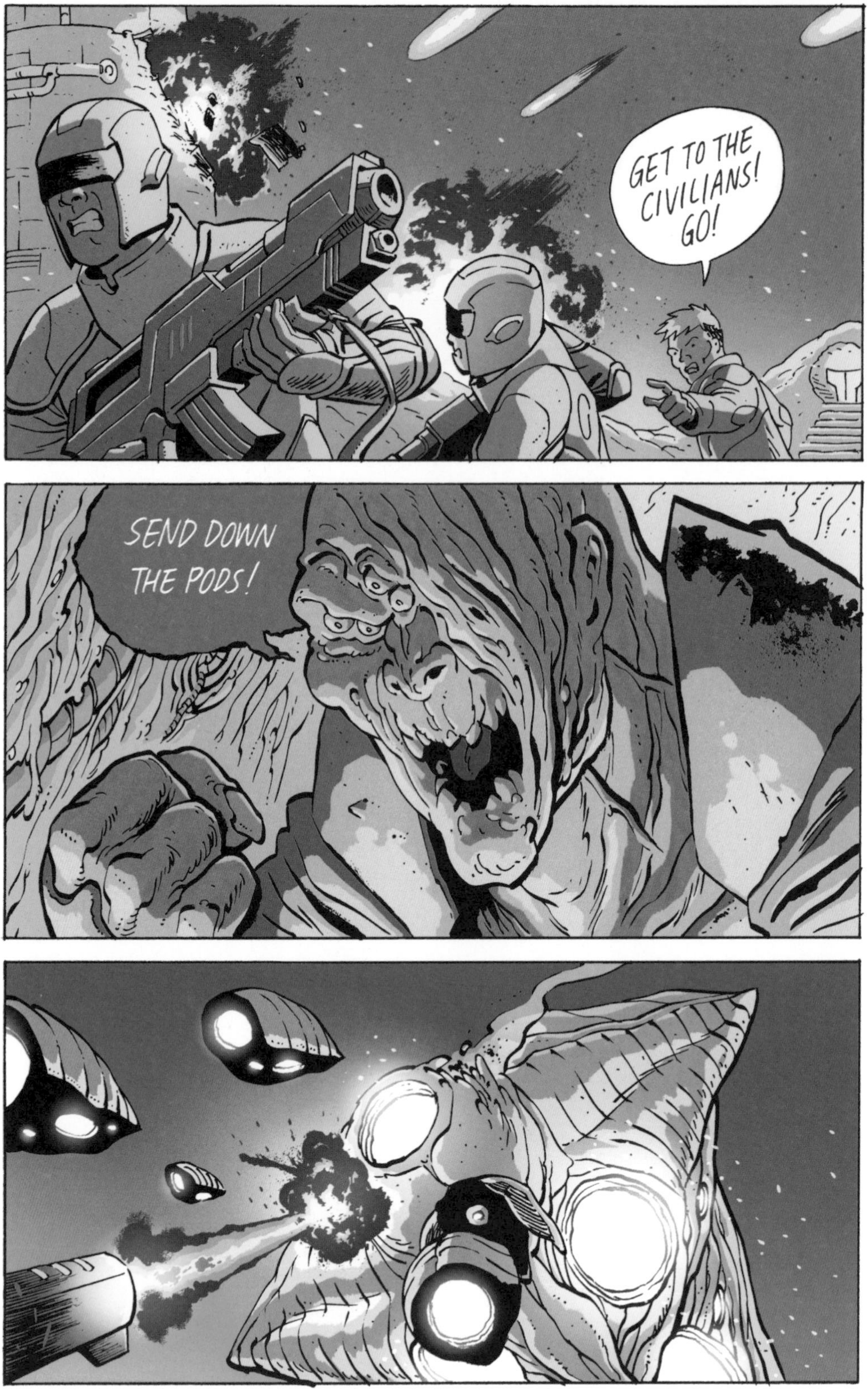
GET TO THE CIVILIANS! GO!
SEND DOWN THE PODS!

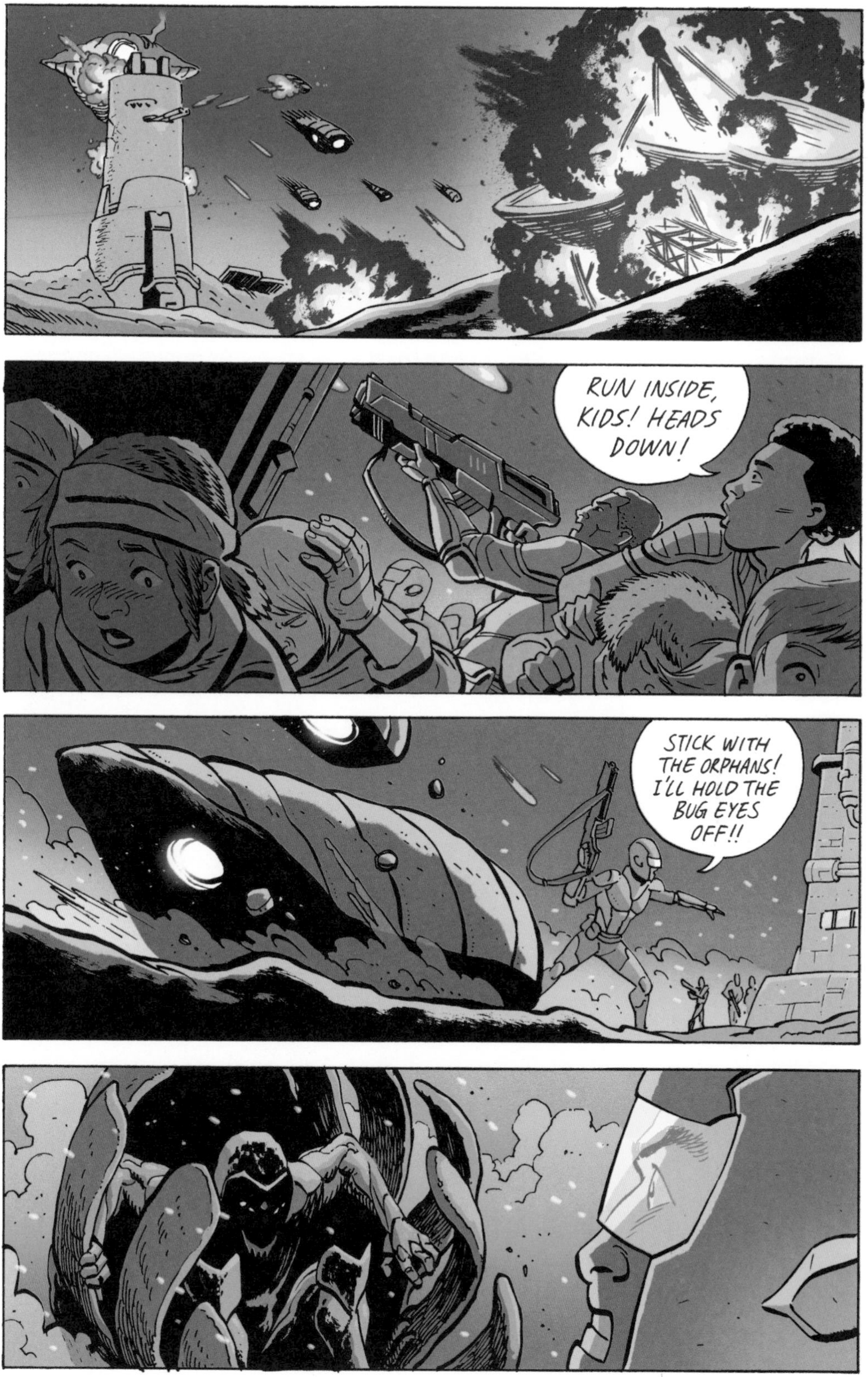
RUN INSIDE, KIDS! HEADS DOWN!
STICK WITH THE ORPHANS! I'LL HOLD THE BUG EYES OFF!!

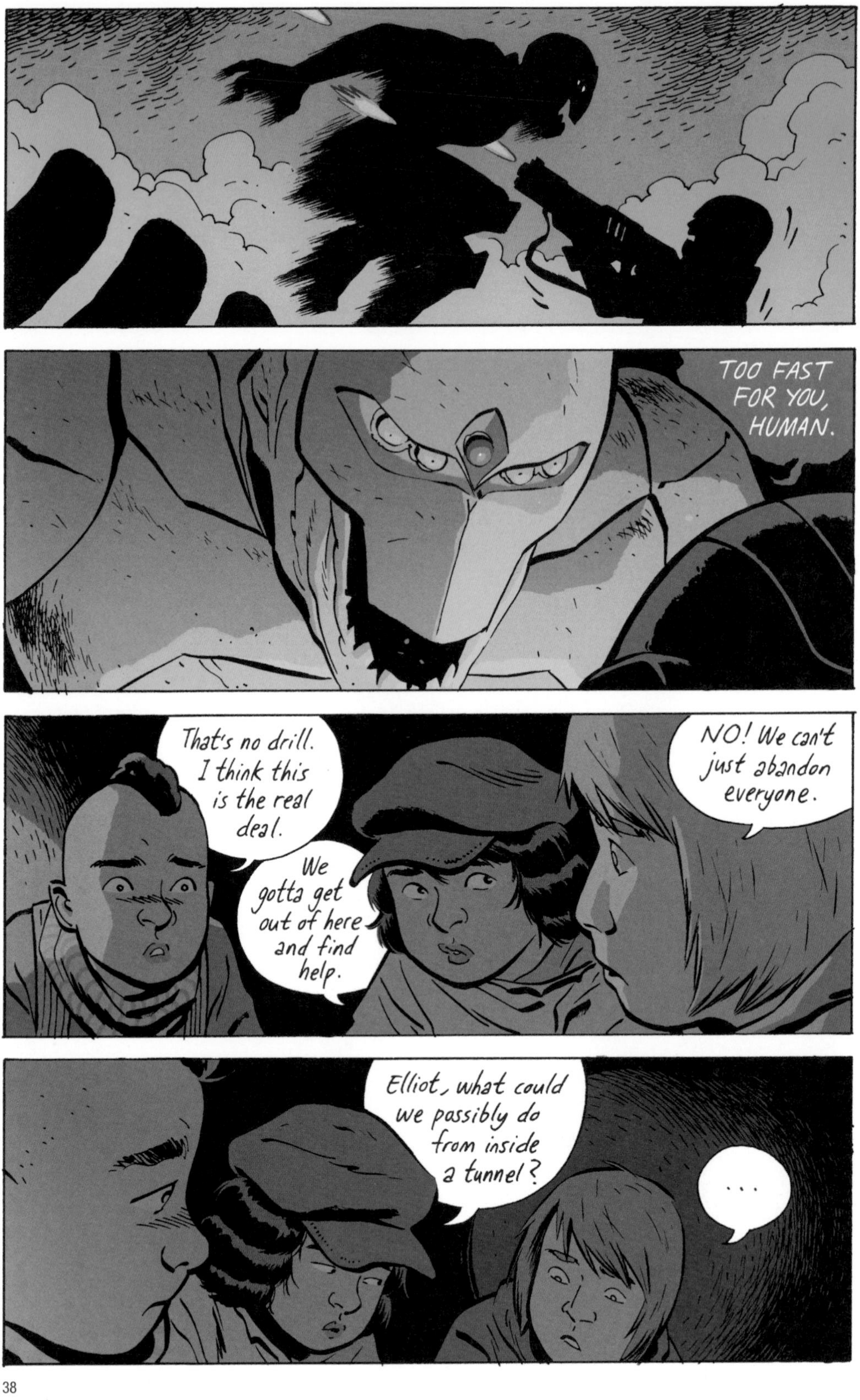
TOO FAST FOR YOU, HUMAN.
That's no drill. I think this is the real deal.
We gotta get out of here and find help.
NO! We can't just abandon everyone.
Elliot, what could we possibly do from inside a tunnel?
...

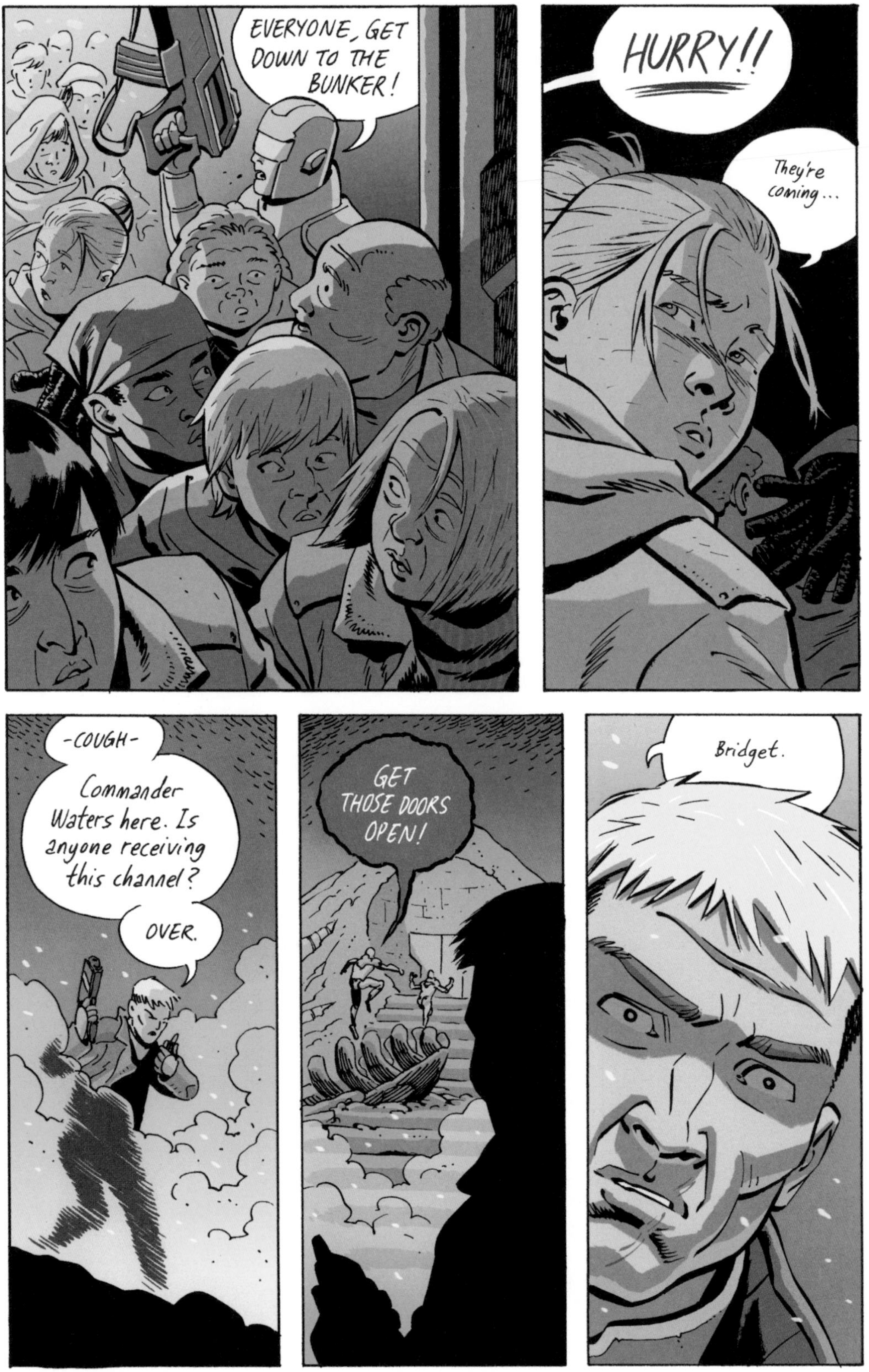
EVERYONE, GET DOWN TO THE BUNKER!
HURRY!!
They're coming...
-COUGH-
Commander Waters here. Is anyone receiving this channel?
OVER.
GET THOSE DOORS OPEN!
Bridget.

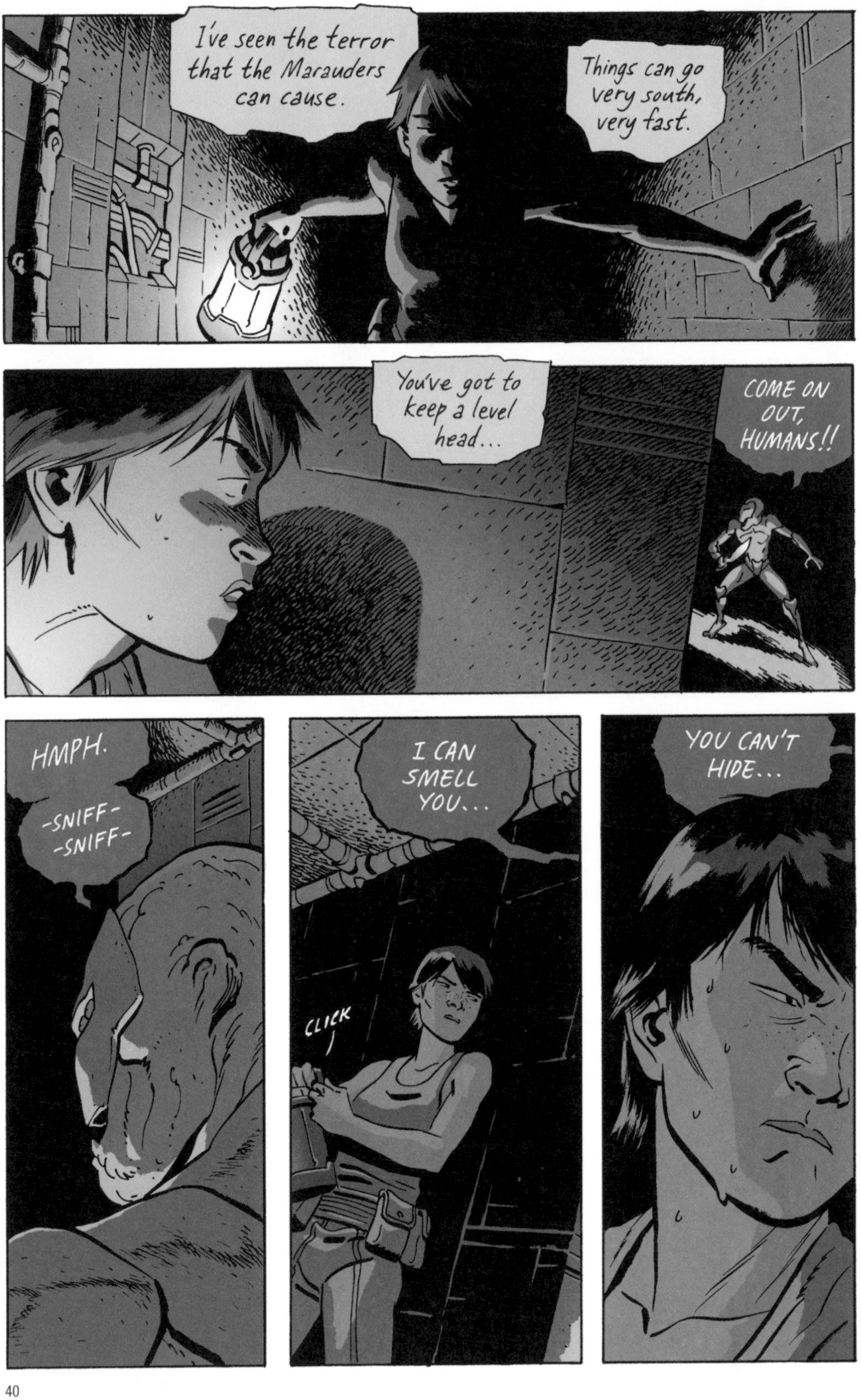
I've seen the terror that the Marauders can cause.
Things can go very south, very fast.
You've got to keep a level head...
COME ON OUT, HUMANS!!
HMPH.
-SNIFF- -SNIFF-
I CAN SMELL YOU...
CLICK
YOU CAN'T HIDE...

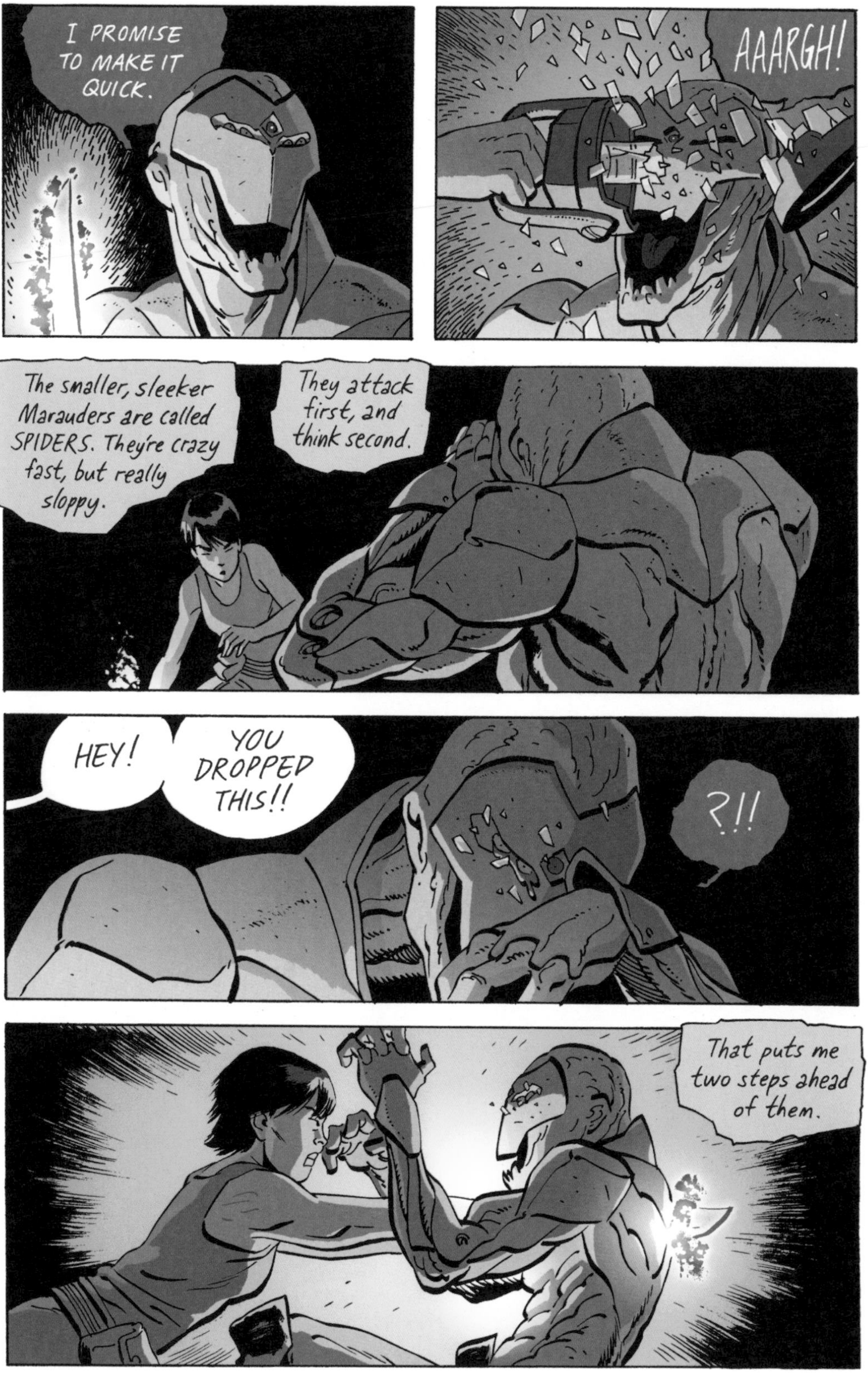
I PROMISE TO MAKE IT QUICK.
AAARGH!
The smaller, sleeker Marauders are called SPIDERS. They're crazy fast, but really sloppy.
They attack first, and think second.
HEY!
YOU DROPPED THIS!!
?!!
That puts me two steps ahead of them.

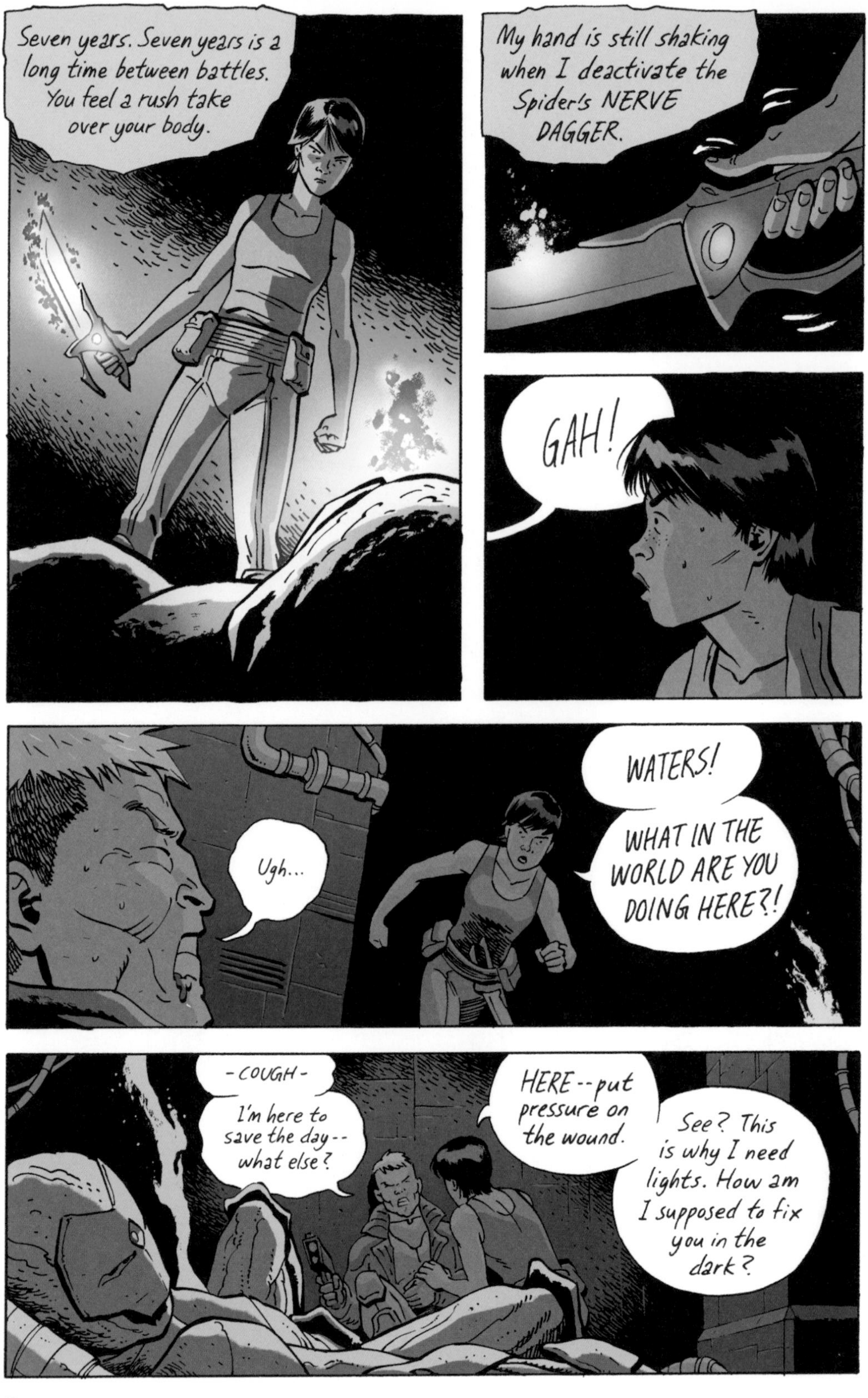
Seven years. Seven years is a long time between battles. You feel a rush take over your body.
My hand is still shaking when I deactivate the Spider's NERVE DAGGER.
GAH!
Ugh...
WATERS!
WHAT IN THE WORLD ARE YOU DOING HERE?!
- COUGH -
I'm here to save the day -- what else?
HERE -- put pressure on the wound.
See? This is why I need lights. How am I supposed to fix you in the dark?

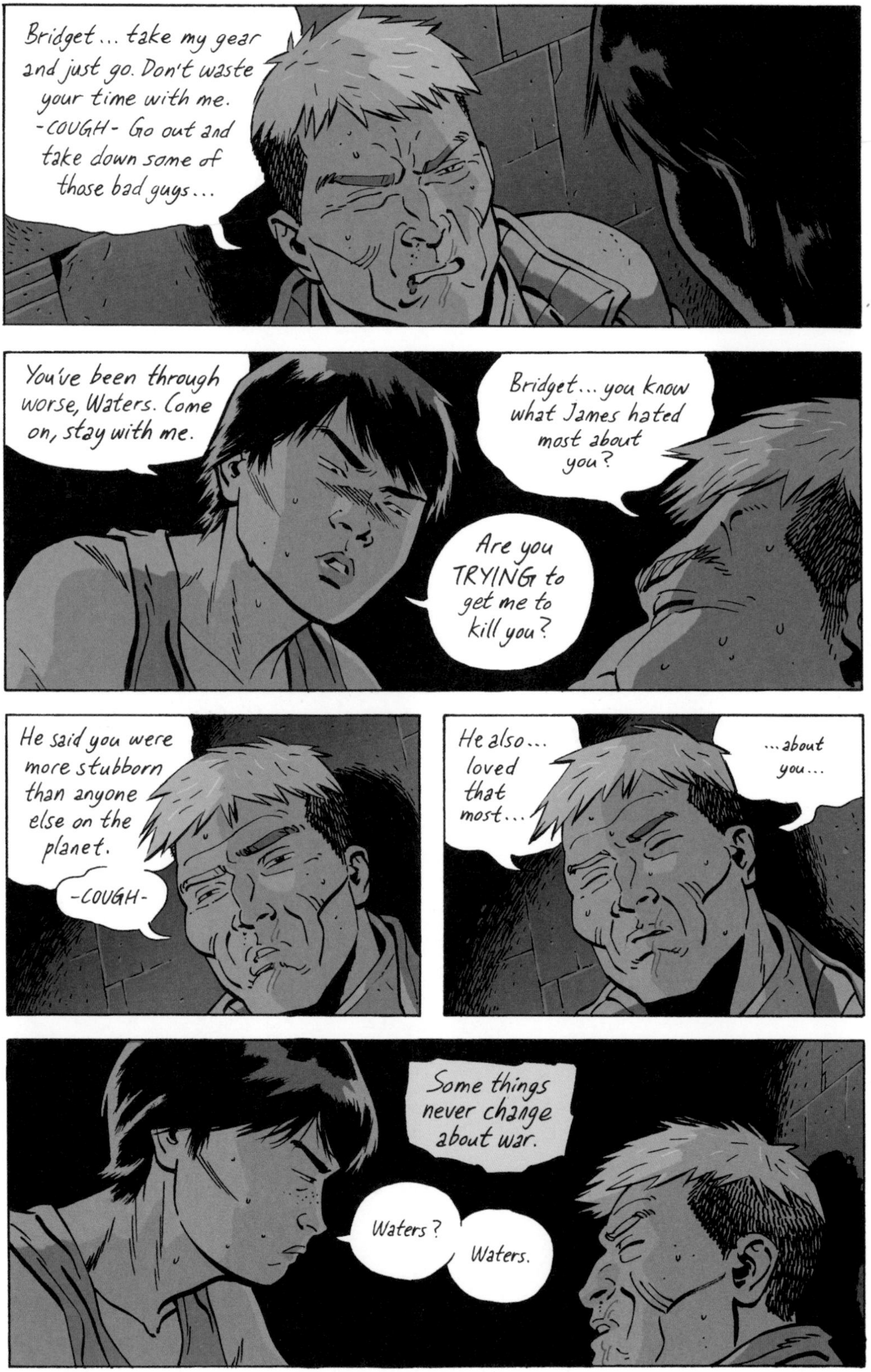
Bridget... take my gear and just go. Don't waste your time with me. -COUGH- Go out and take down some of those bad guys...
You've been through worse, Waters. Come on, stay with me.
Bridget... you know what James hated most about you?
Are you TRYING to get me to kill you?
He said you were more stubborn than anyone else on the planet.
-COUGH-
He also... loved that most...
...about you...
Some things never change about war.
Waters?
Waters.

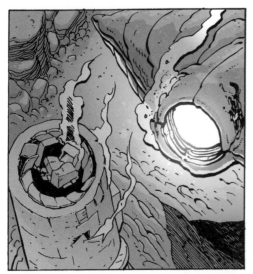

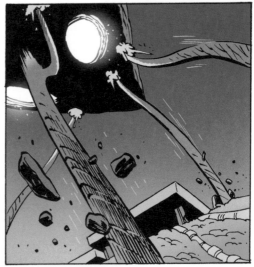

It's--it's HALF-FACE! THE MAD GENERAL!

MAD? OH, I'M DELIRIOUS.

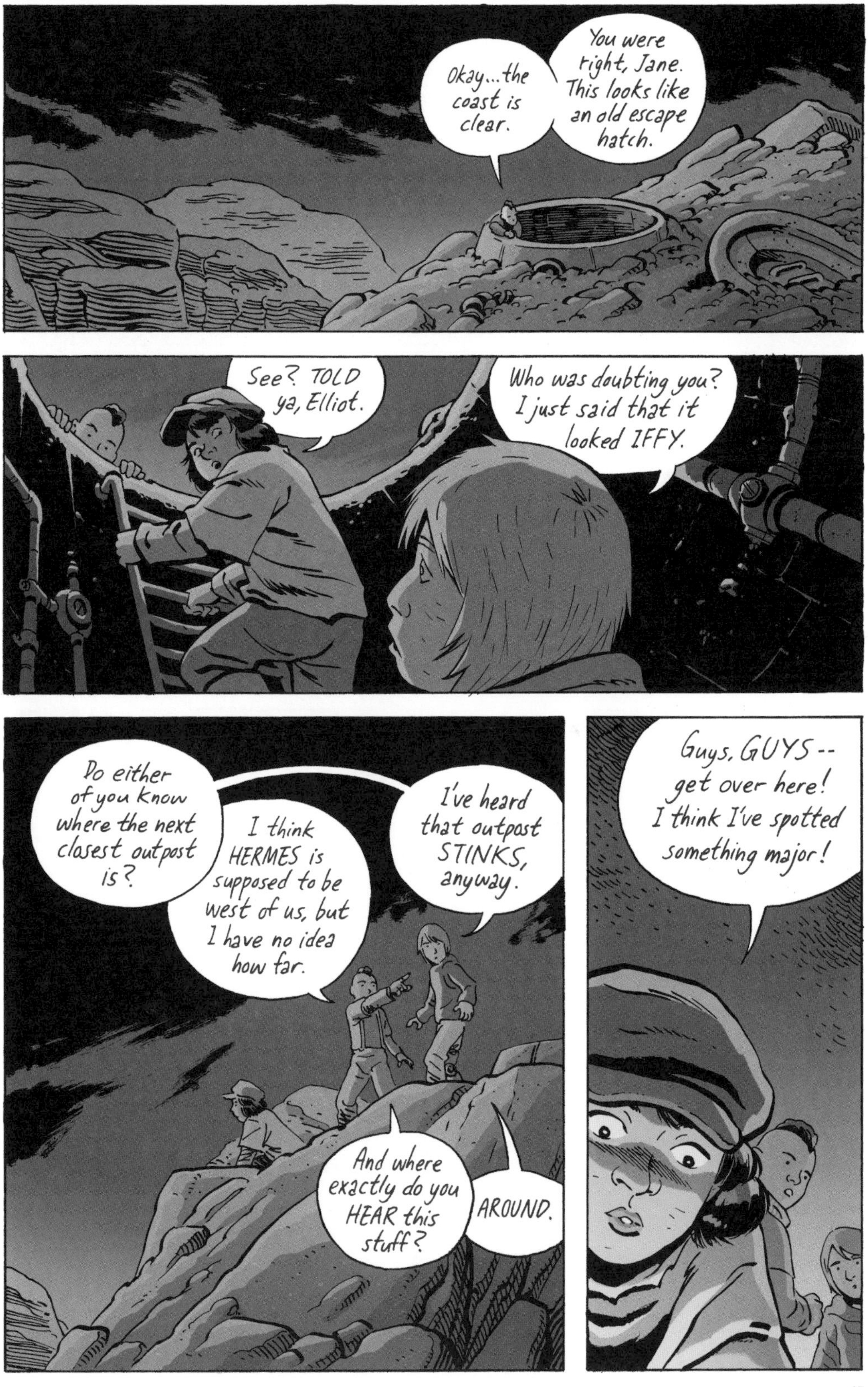
Okay... the coast is clear.
You were right, Jane. This looks like an old escape hatch.
See? TOLD ya, Elliot.
Who was doubting you? I just said that it looked IFFY.
Do either of you know where the next closest outpost is?
I think HERMES is supposed to be west of us, but I have no idea how far.
I've heard that outpost STINKS, anyway.
And where exactly do you HEAR this stuff?
AROUND.
Guys, GUYS -- get over here! I think I've spotted something major!

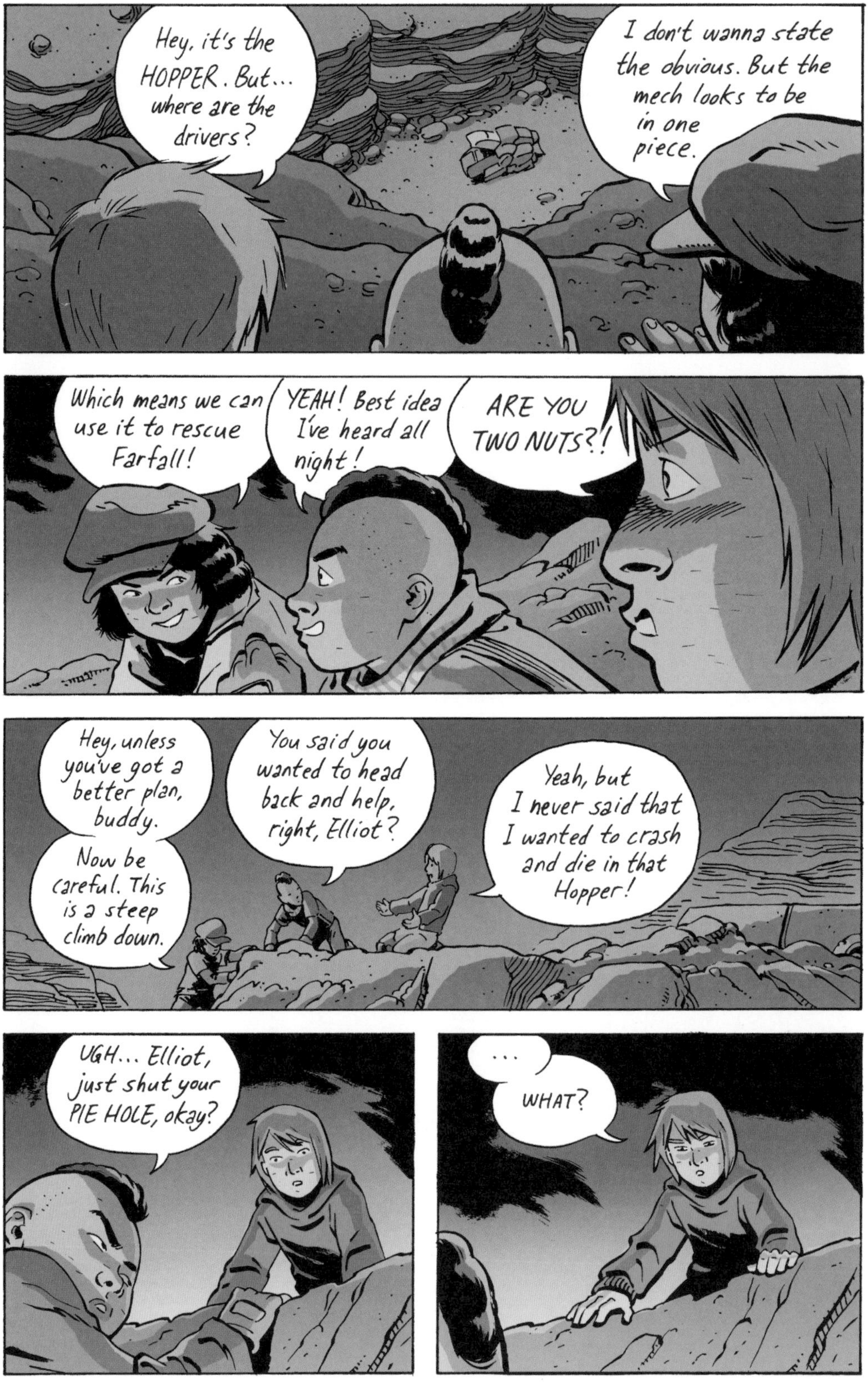
Hey, it's the HOPPER. But... where are the drivers?
I don't wanna state the obvious. But the mech looks to be in one piece.
Which means we can use it to rescue Farfall!
YEAH! Best idea I've heard all night!
ARE YOU TWO NUTS?!
Hey, unless you've got a better plan, buddy.
Now be careful. This is a steep climb down.
You said you wanted to head back and help, right, Elliot?
Yeah, but I never said that I wanted to crash and die in that Hopper!
UGH... Elliot, just shut your PIE HOLE, okay?
...
WHAT?

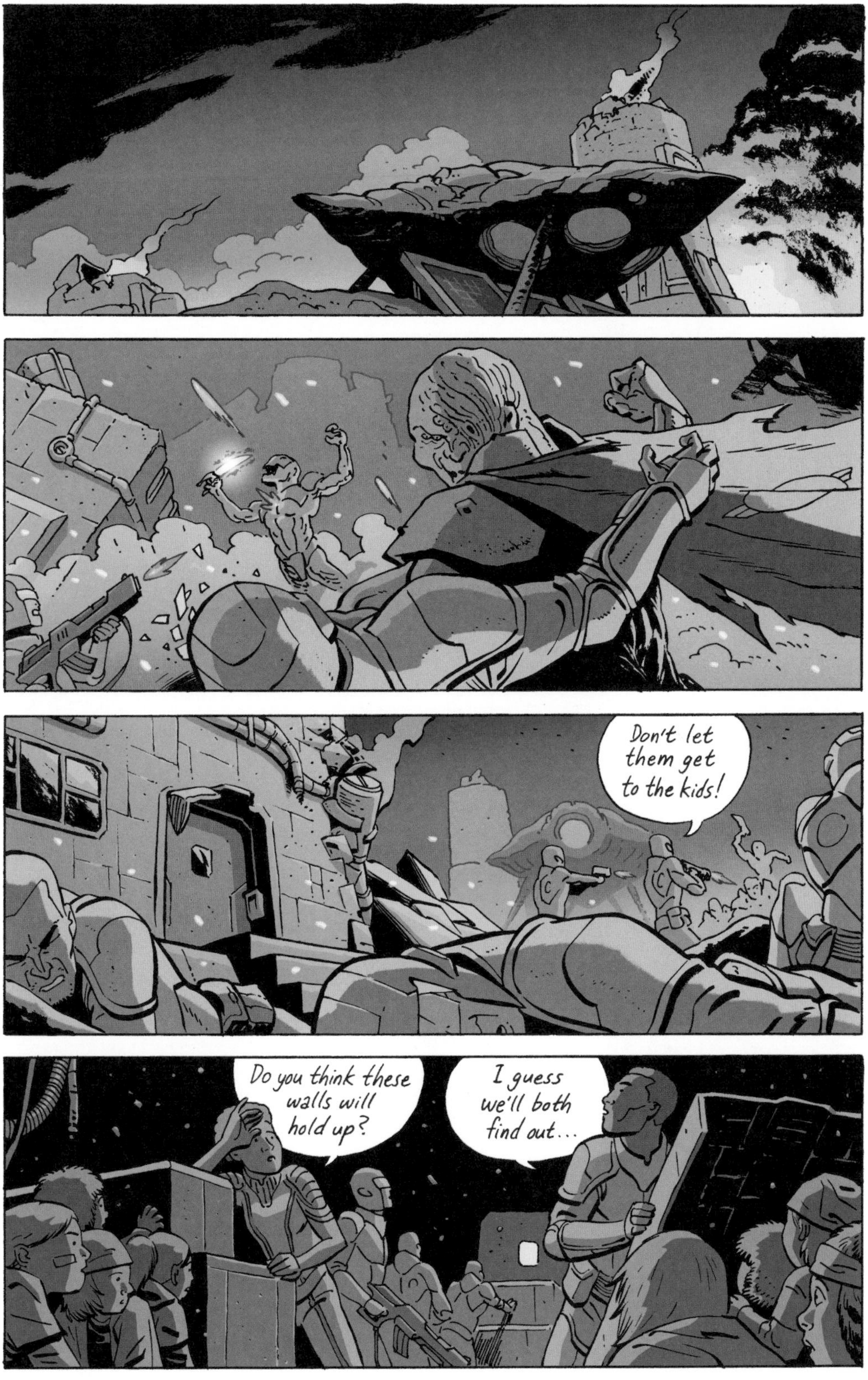
Don't let them get to the kids!
Do you think these walls will hold up?
I guess we'll both find out...

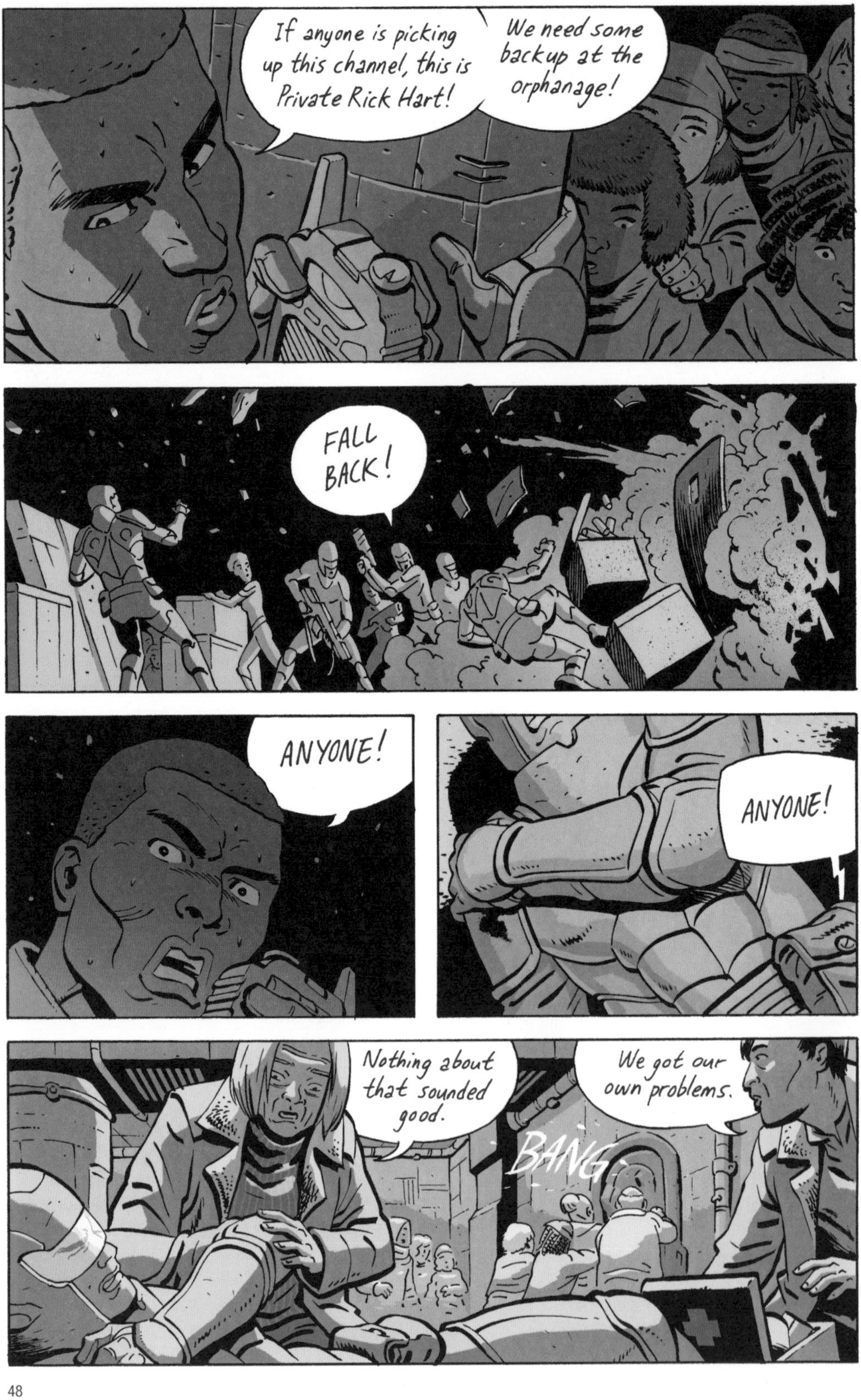
If anyone is picking up this channel, this is Private Rick Hart!
We need some backup at the orphanage!
FALL BACK!
ANYONE!
ANYONE!
Nothing about that sounded good.
We got our own problems.
BANG

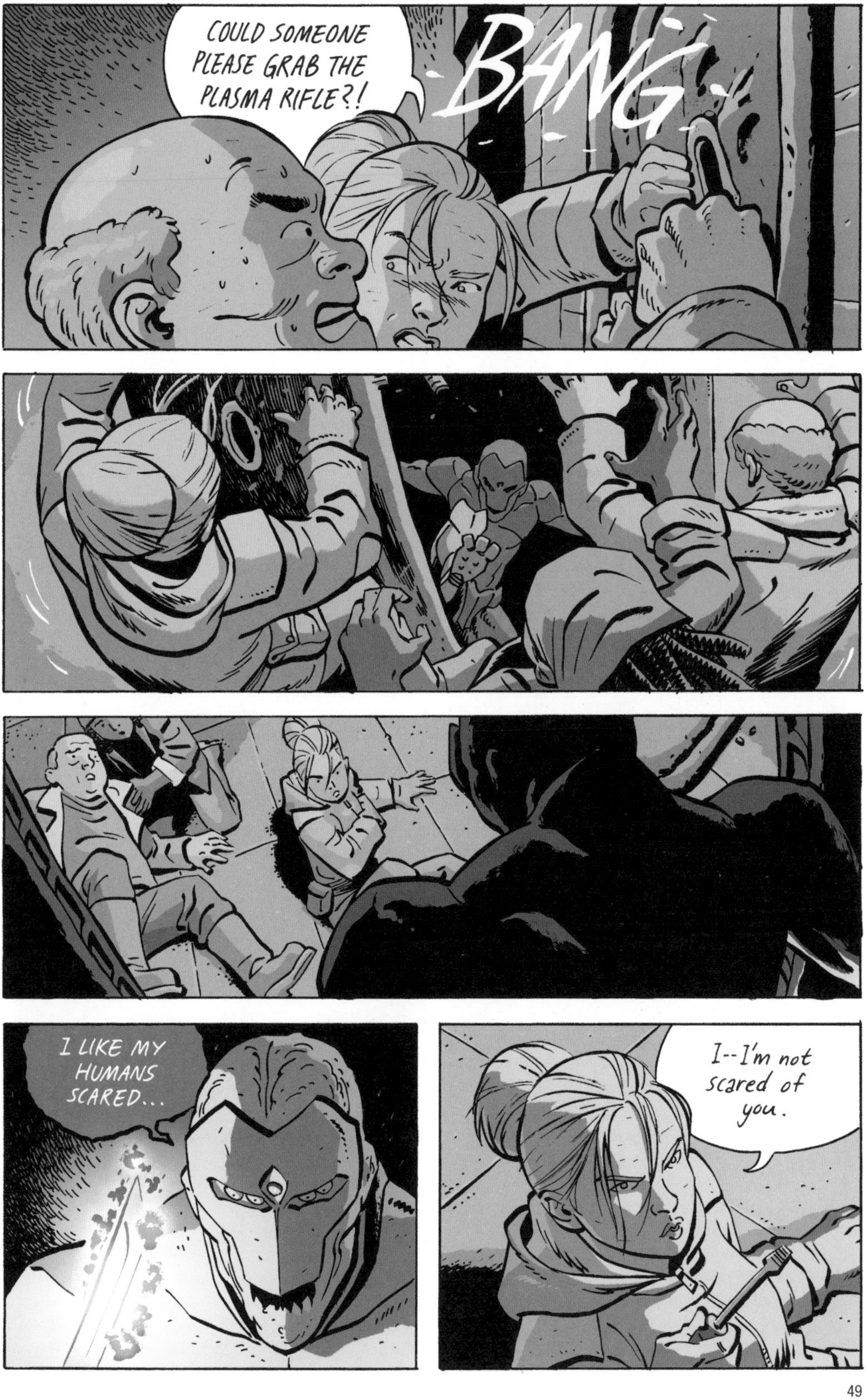
COULD SOMEONE PLEASE GRAB THE PLASMA RIFLE?!
BANG
I LIKE MY HUMANS SCARED...
I--I'm not scared of you.

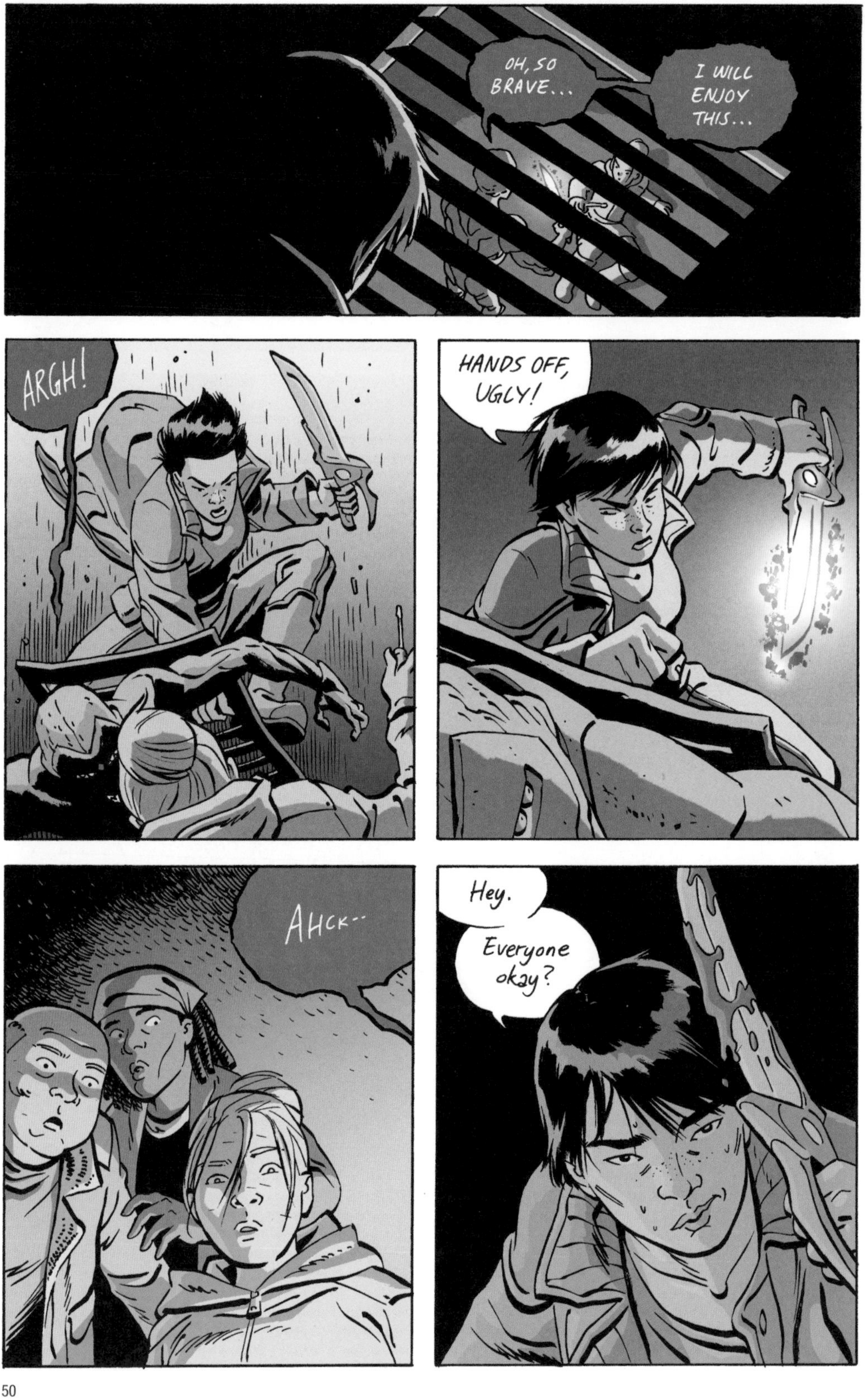
OH, SO BRAVE...
I WILL ENJOY THIS...
ARGH!
HANDS OFF, UGLY!
AHCK--
Hey.
Everyone okay?

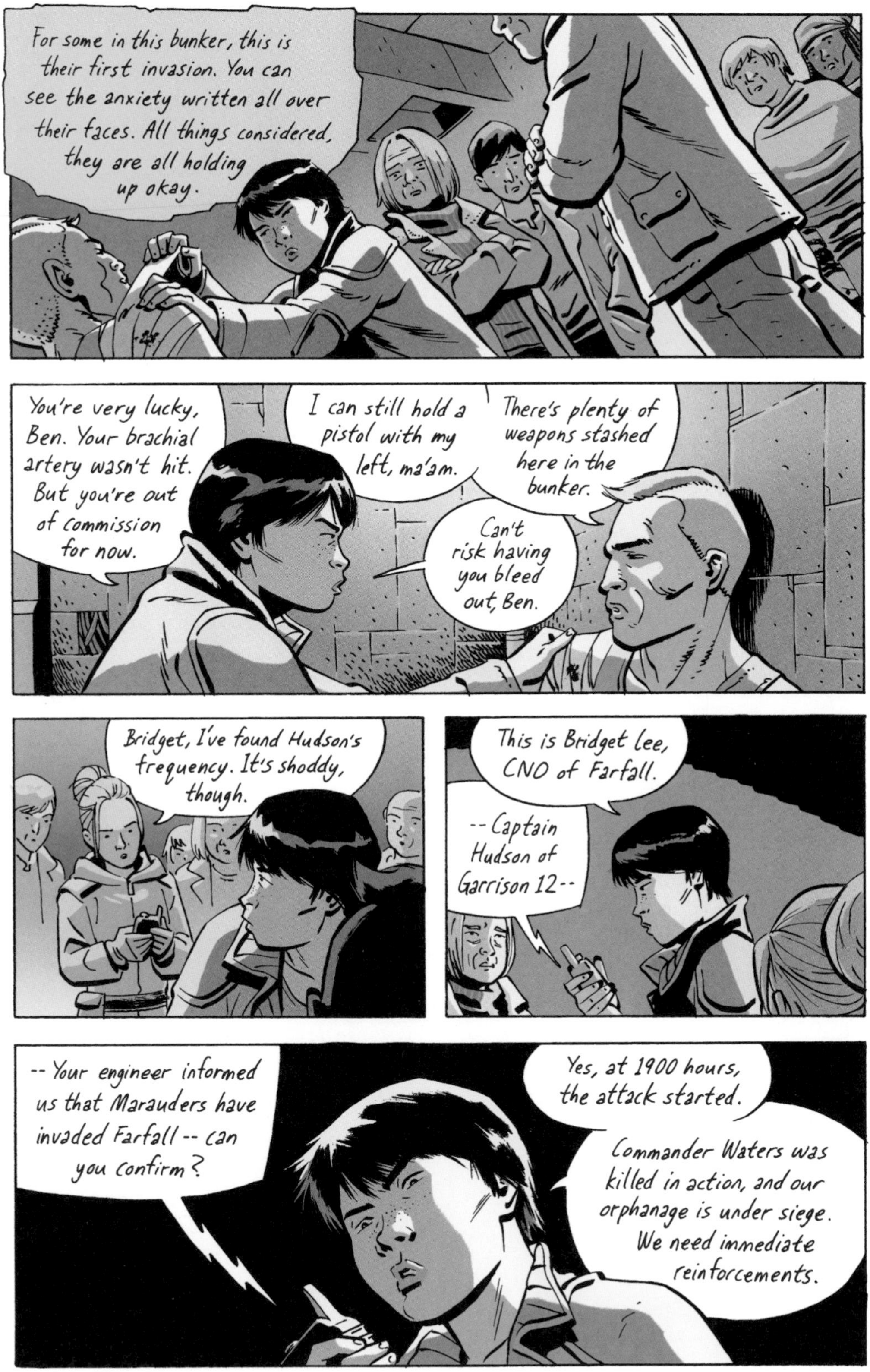
For some in this bunker, this is their first invasion. You can see the anxiety written all over their faces. All things considered, they are all holding up okay.
You're very lucky, Ben. Your brachial artery wasn't hit. But you're out of commission for now.
I can still hold a pistol with my left, ma'am.
There's plenty of weapons stashed here in the bunker.
Can't risk having you bleed out, Ben.
Bridget, I've found Hudson's frequency. It's shoddy, though.
This is Bridget Lee, CNO of Farfall.
--Captain Hudson of Garrison 12--
--Your engineer informed us that Marauders have invaded Farfall -- can you confirm?
Yes, at 1900 hours, the attack started.
Commander Waters was killed in action, and our orphanage is under siege. We need immediate reinforcements.

--NEGATIVE, Lee. Any reinforcements will be in vain -- the Marauders will overrun Farfall before dawn -- I can't send my men into a deathtrap --

Captain, we can't just LEAVE the orphans to be captured.

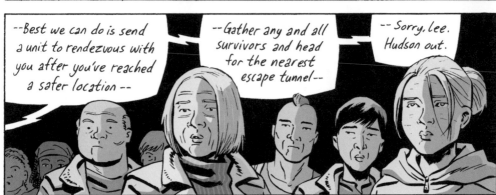

--Best we can do is send a unit to rendezvous with you after you've reached a safer location --

--Gather any and all survivors and head for the nearest escape tunnel--

-- Sorry, Lee. Hudson out.

Well, that was a big bag of nothing.

Bree... I think I might have a plan. You up for some danger?

Well, when you put it like THAT, Bridget...

You going to rescue the orphans?

If so, we're coming with you.

Zhan, if you really enjoy BREATHING, I'd seriously advise against that. You all stay in this bunker.

No, Bridget.

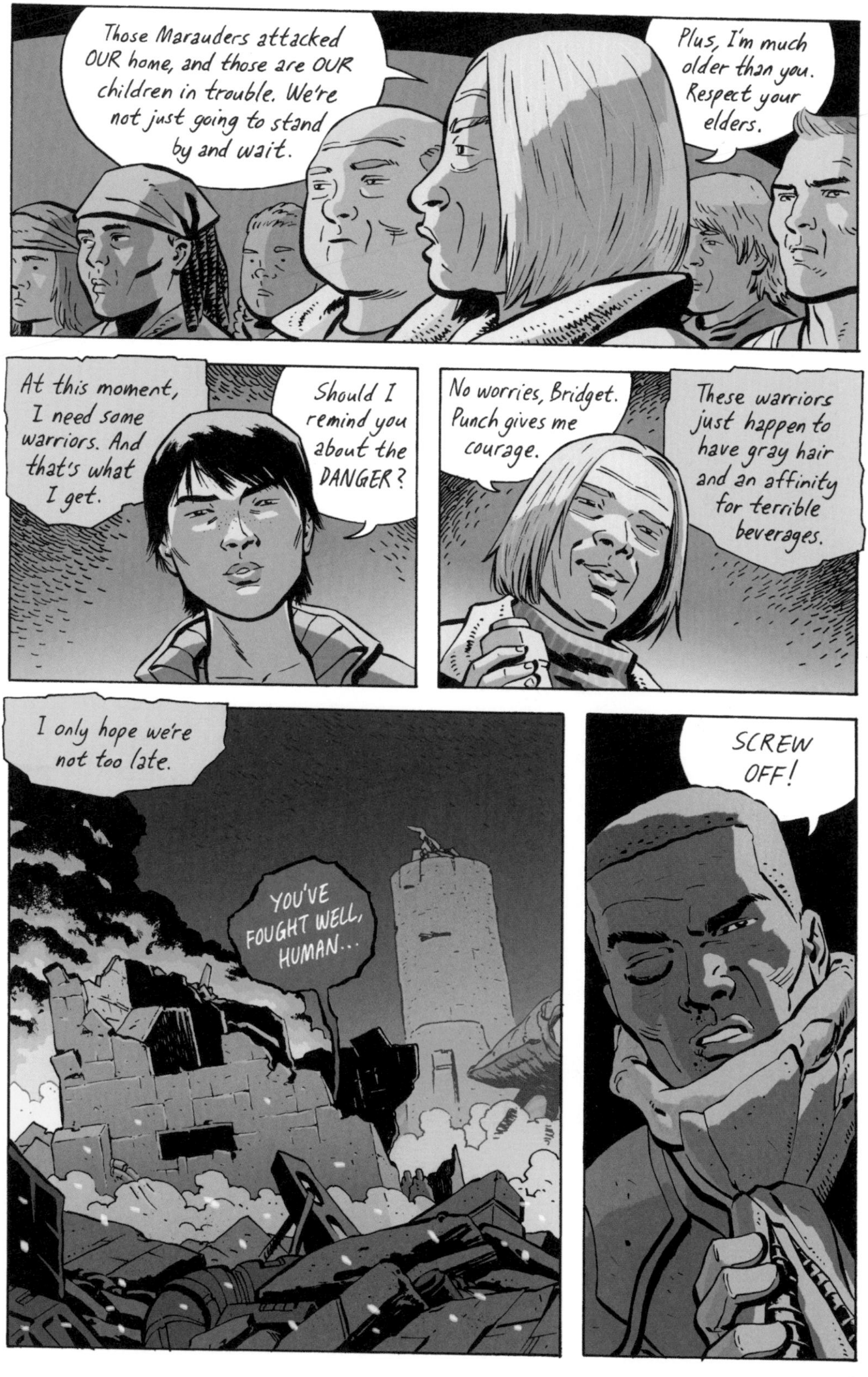
Those Marauders attacked OUR home, and those are OUR children in trouble. We're not just going to stand by and wait.
Plus, I'm much older than you. Respect your elders.
At this moment, I need some warriors. And that's what I get.
Should I remind you about the DANGER?
No worries, Bridget. Punch gives me courage.
These warriors just happen to have gray hair and an affinity for terrible beverages.
I only hope we're not too late.
YOU'VE FOUGHT WELL, HUMAN...
SCREW OFF!

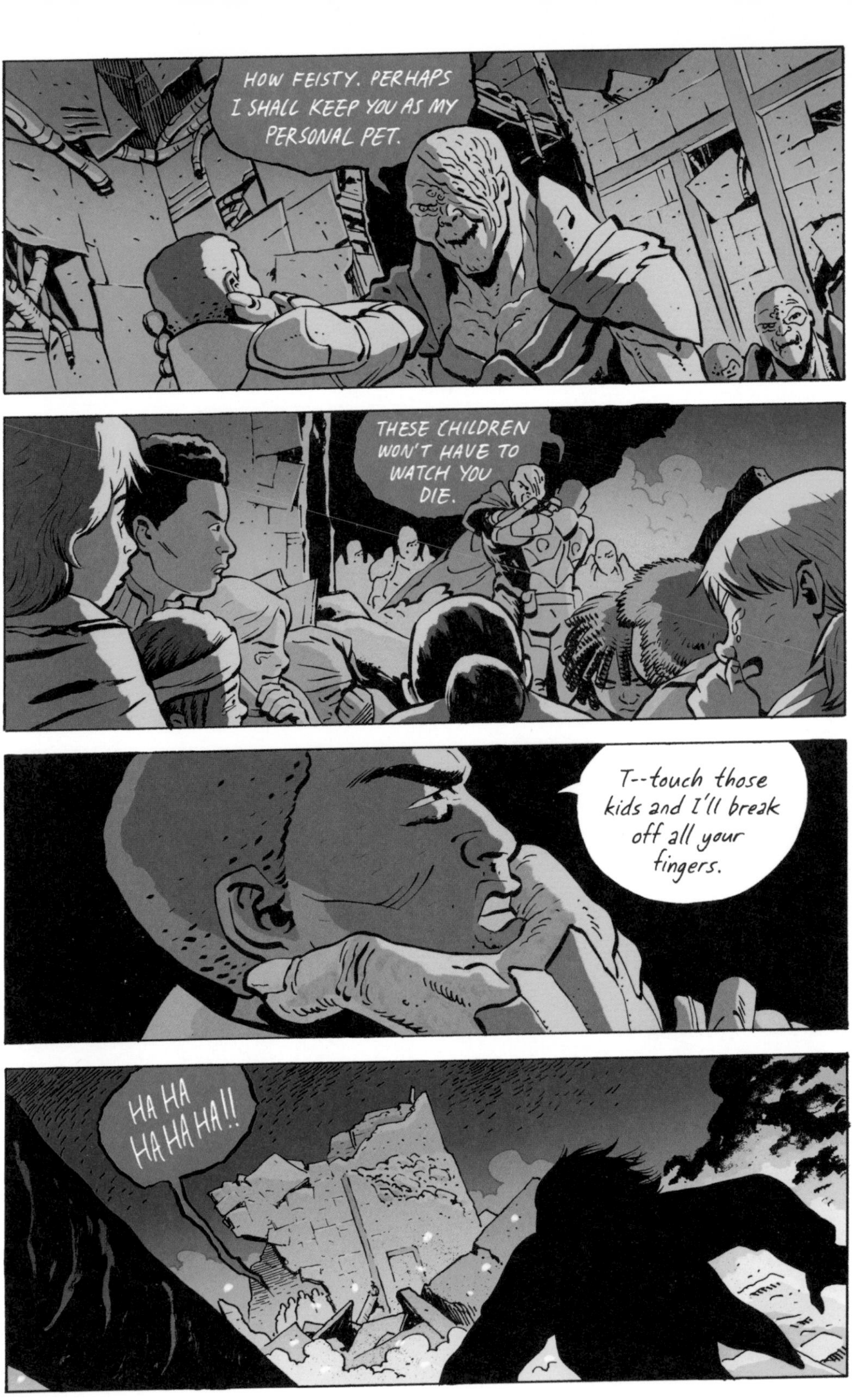
HOW FEISTY. PERHAPS I SHALL KEEP YOU AS MY PERSONAL PET.
THESE CHILDREN WON'T HAVE TO WATCH YOU DIE.
T--touch those kids and I'll break off all your fingers.
HA HA HA HA HA!!

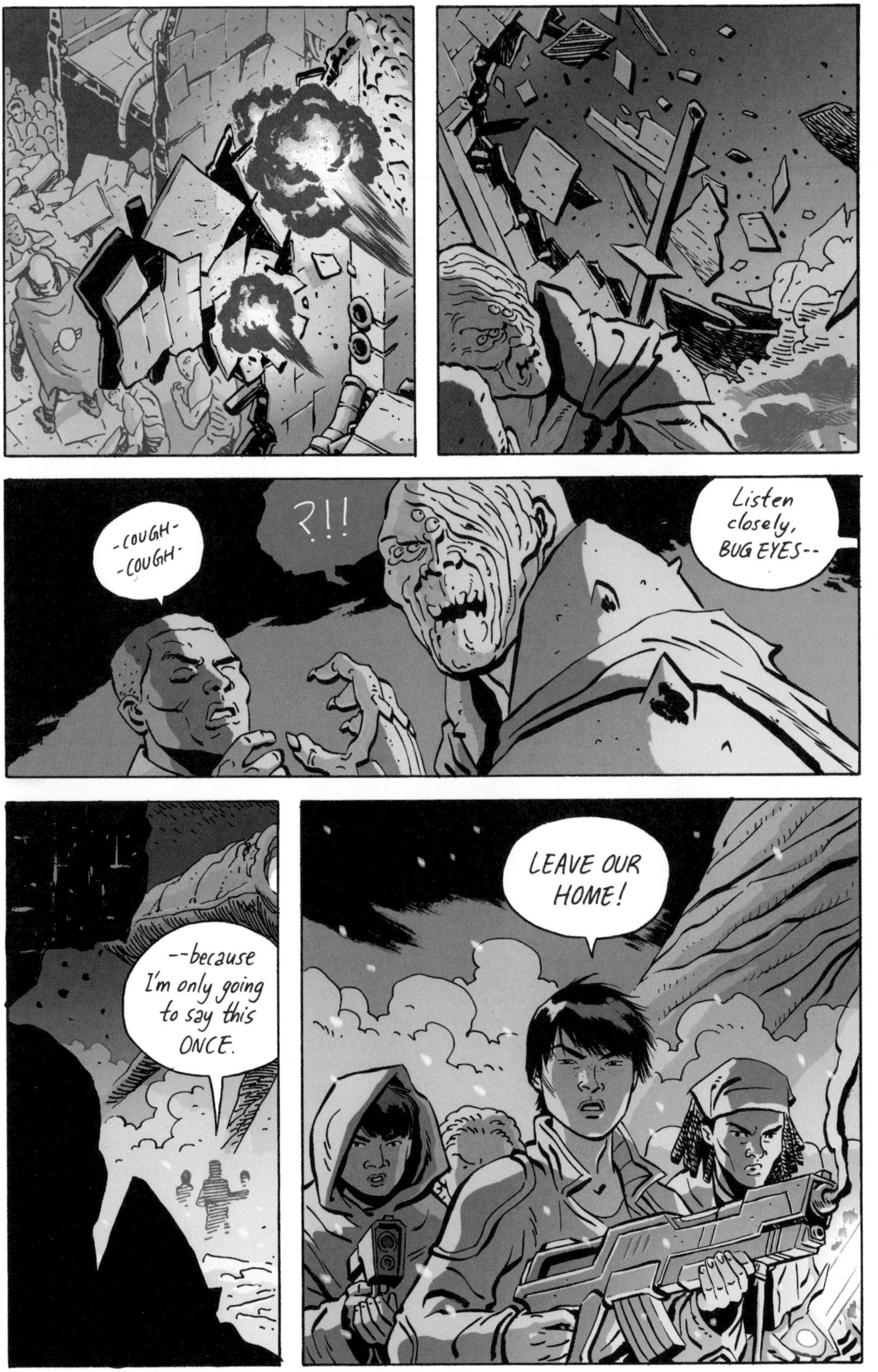
?!!
-COUGH-
-COUGH-
Listen closely, BUG EYES--
--because I'm only going to say this ONCE.
LEAVE OUR HOME!

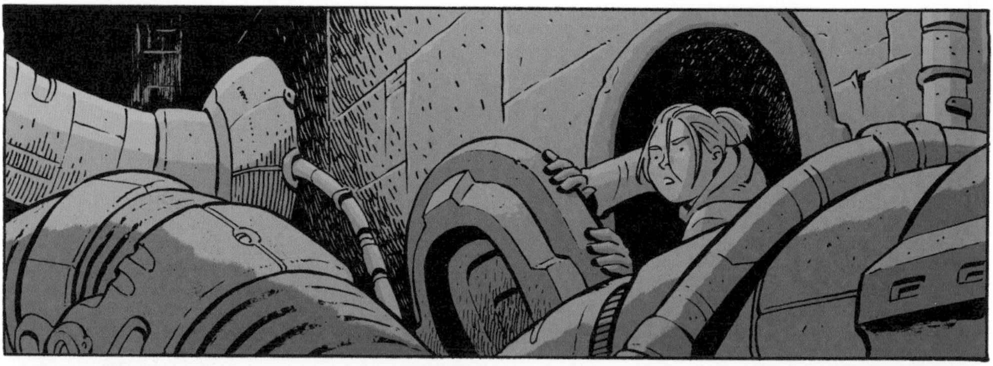

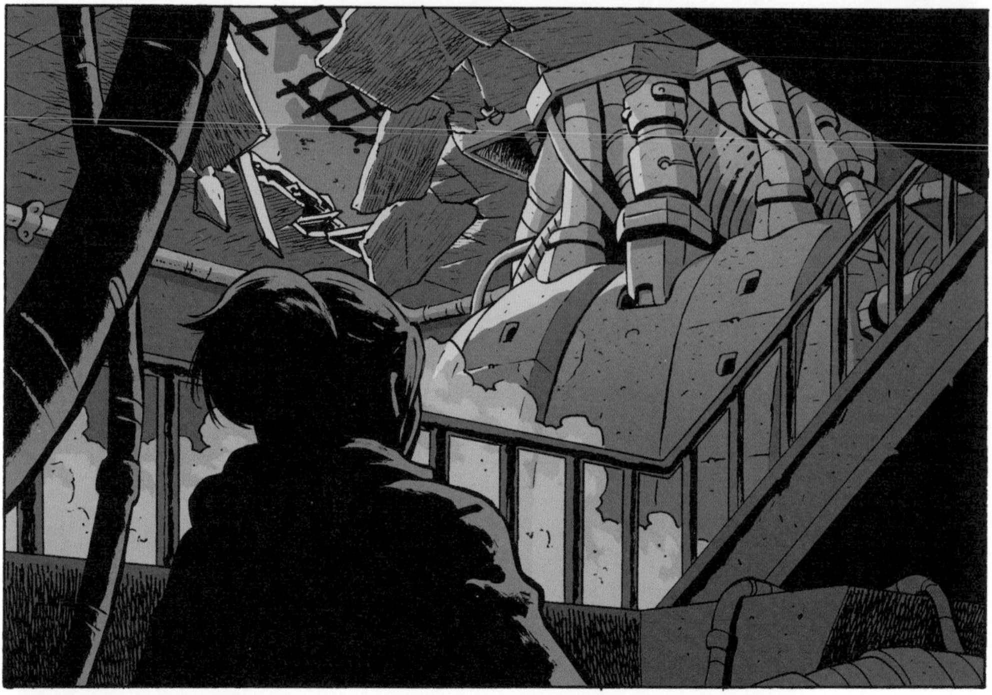

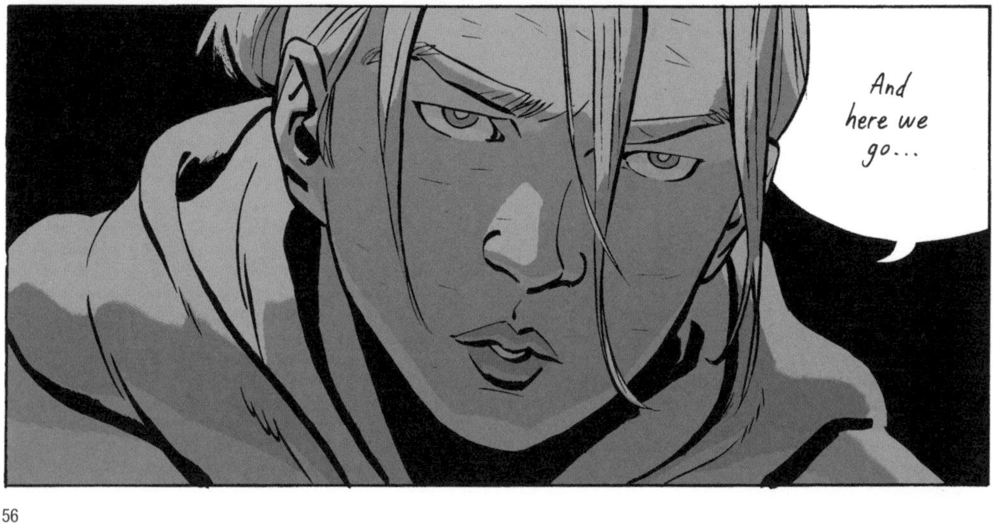
And here we go...

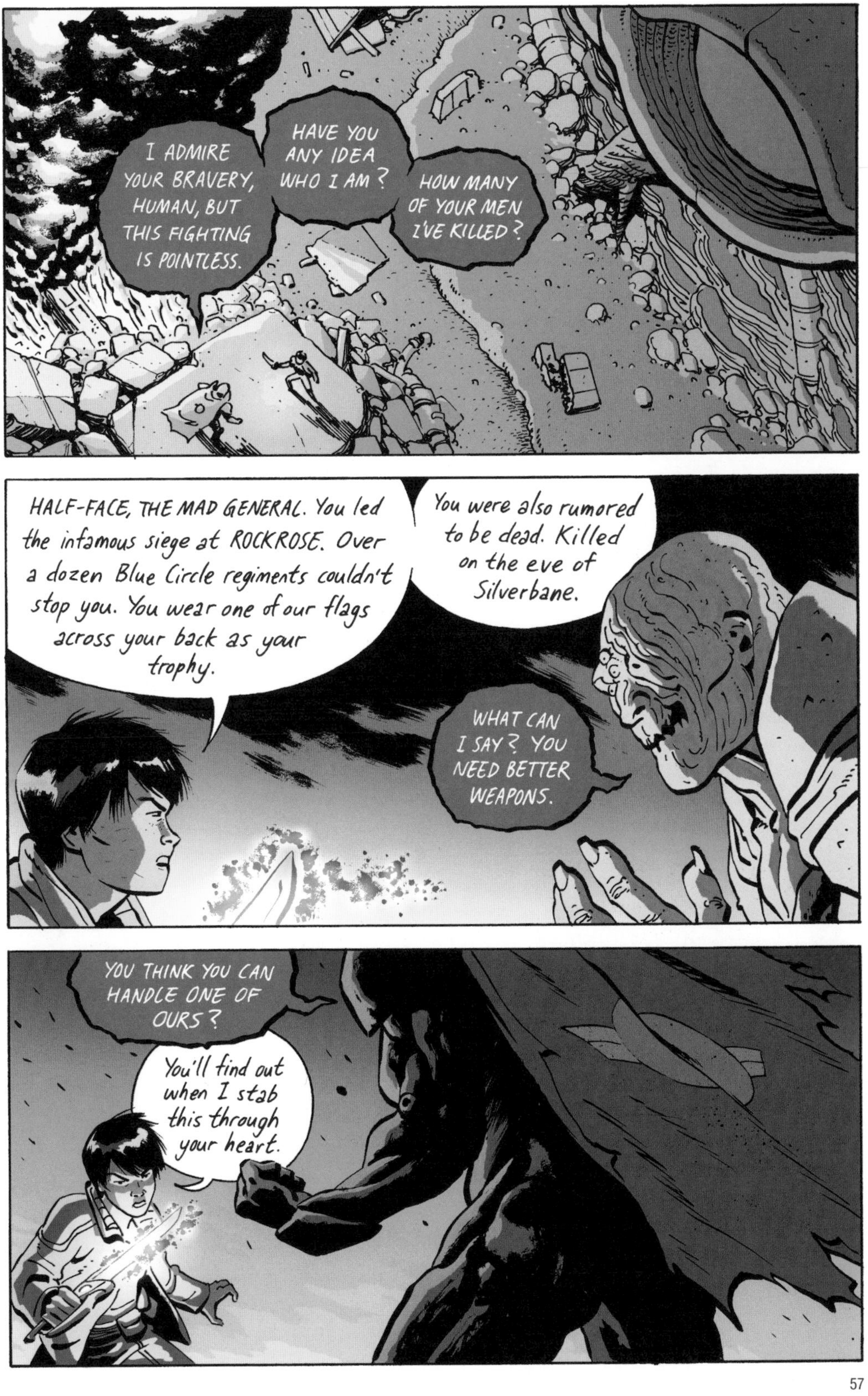
I ADMIRE YOUR BRAVERY, HUMAN, BUT THIS FIGHTING IS POINTLESS.
HAVE YOU ANY IDEA WHO I AM?
HOW MANY OF YOUR MEN I'VE KILLED?
HALF-FACE, THE MAD GENERAL. You led the infamous siege at ROCKROSE. Over a dozen Blue Circle regiments couldn't stop you. You wear one of our flags across your back as your trophy.
You were also rumored to be dead. Killed on the eve of Silverbane.
WHAT CAN I SAY? YOU NEED BETTER WEAPONS.
YOU THINK YOU CAN HANDLE ONE OF OURS?
You'll find out when I stab this through your heart.

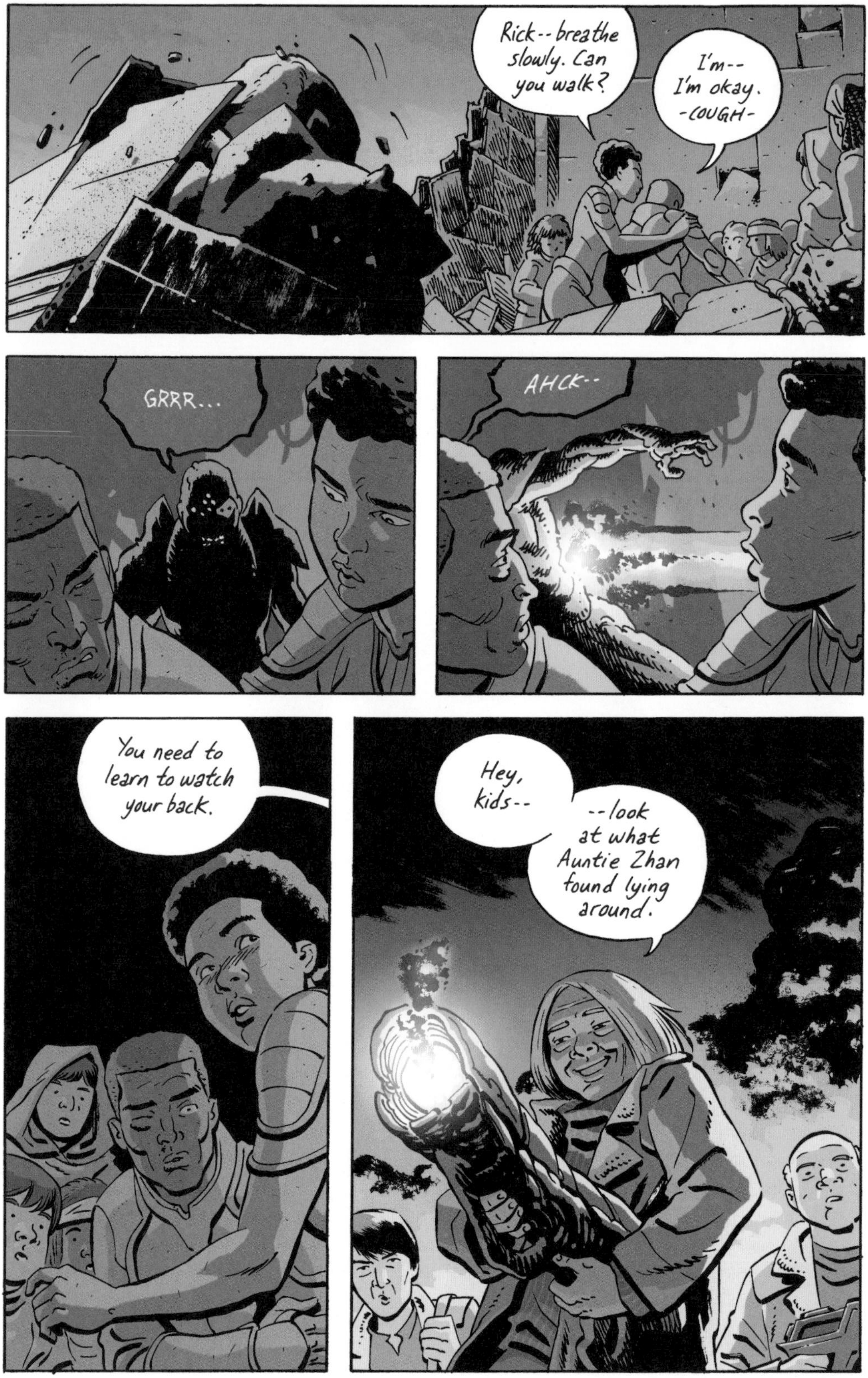
Rick--breathe slowly. Can you walk?
I'm-- I'm okay. -COUGH-
GRRR...
AHCK--
You need to learn to watch your back.
Hey, kids--
--look at what Auntie Zhan found lying around.

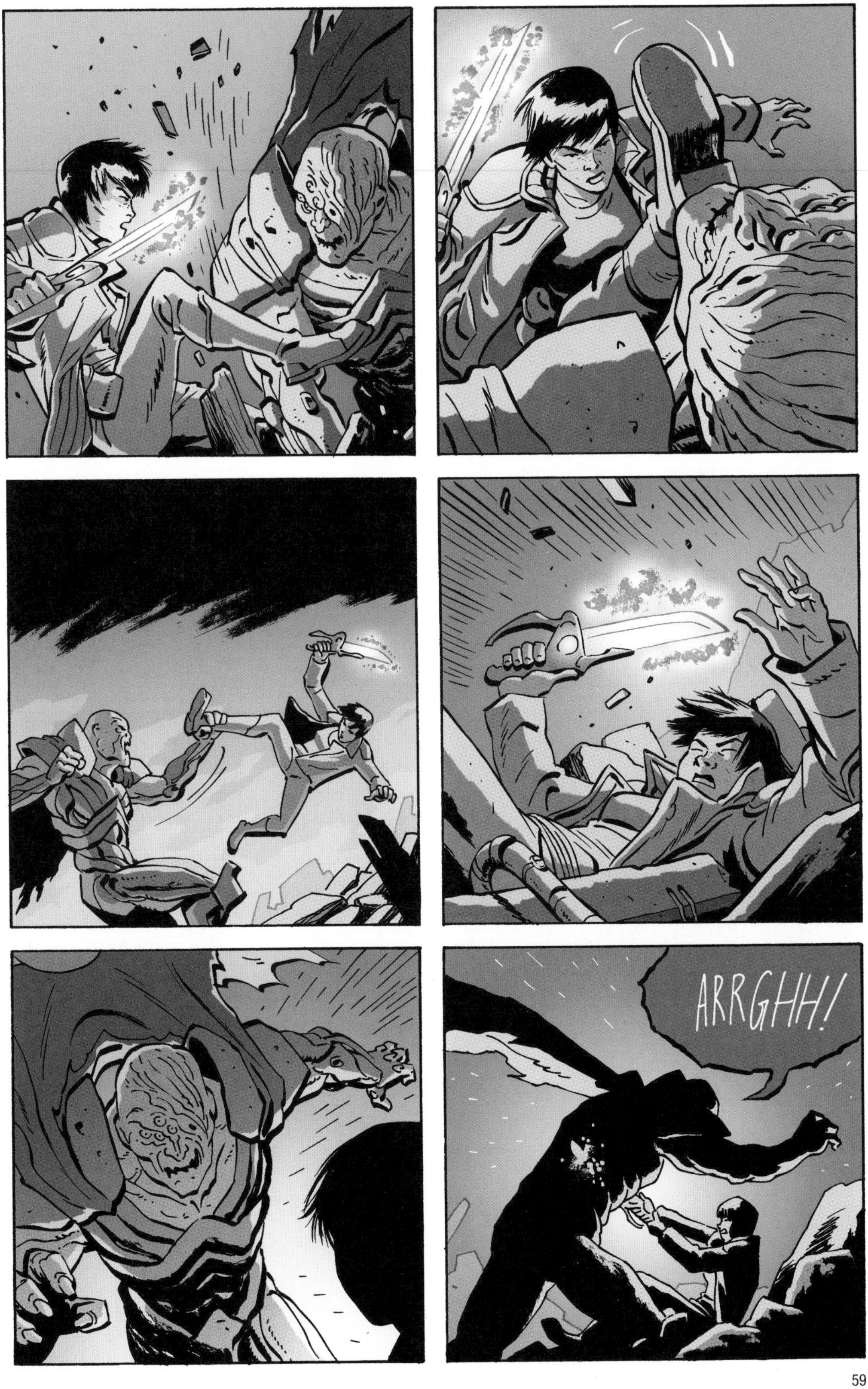
ARRGHH!

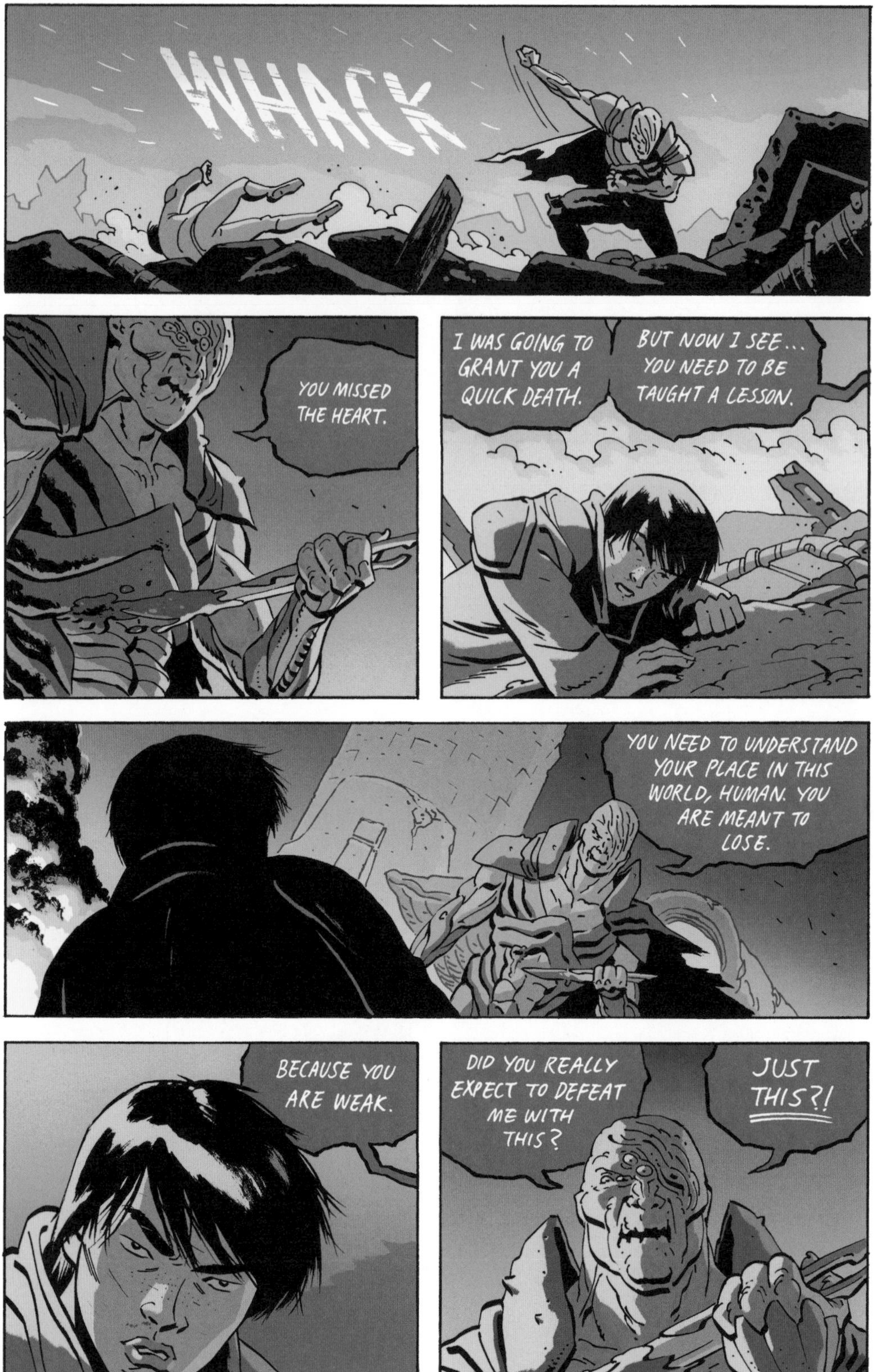
WHACK
YOU MISSED THE HEART.
I WAS GOING TO GRANT YOU A QUICK DEATH.
BUT NOW I SEE... YOU NEED TO BE TAUGHT A LESSON.
YOU NEED TO UNDERSTAND YOUR PLACE IN THIS WORLD, HUMAN. YOU ARE MEANT TO LOSE.
BECAUSE YOU ARE WEAK.
DID YOU REALLY EXPECT TO DEFEAT ME WITH THIS?
JUST THIS?!

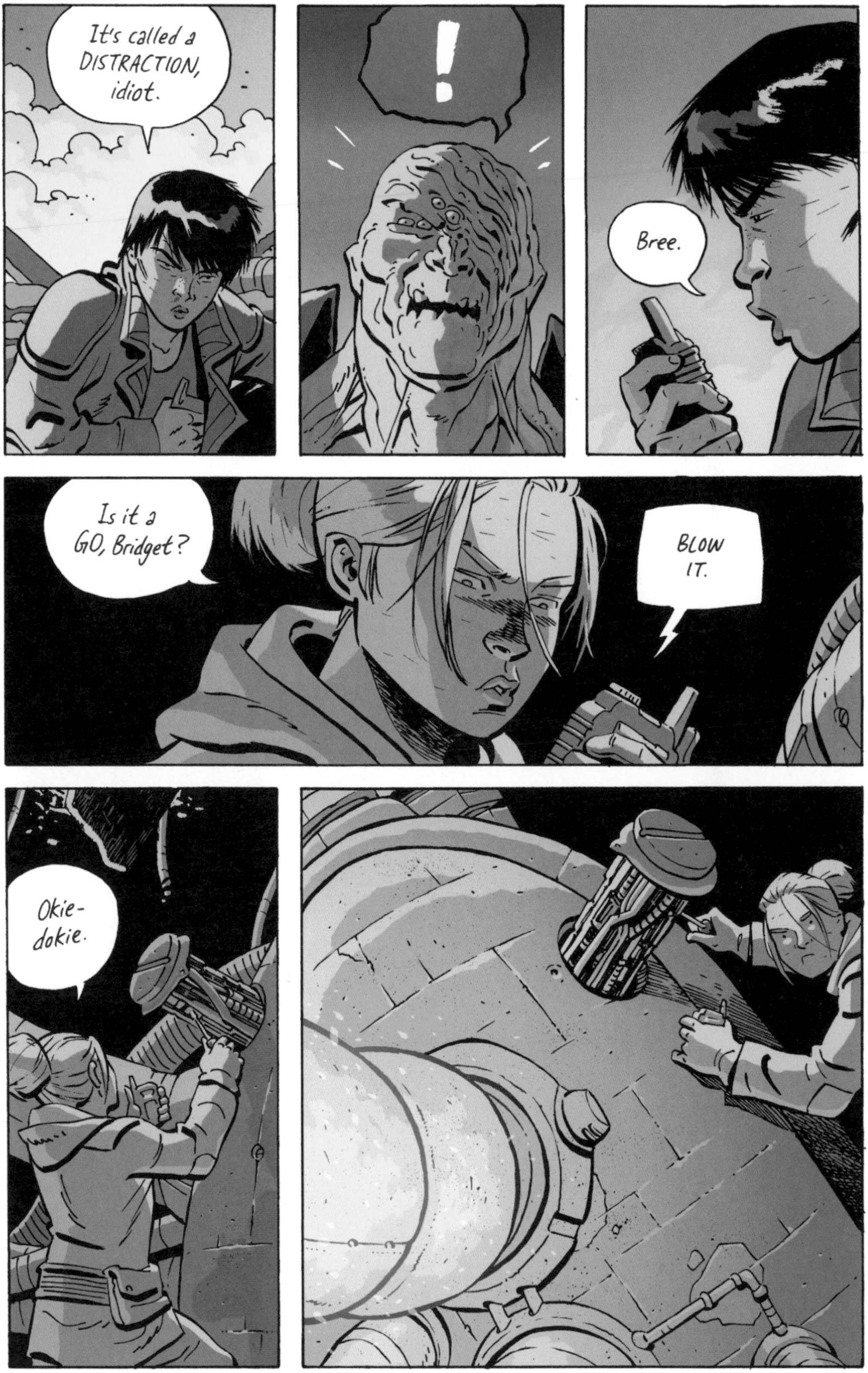
It's called a DISTRACTION, idiot.
!
Bree.
Is it a GO, Bridget?
BLOW IT.
Okie-dokie.

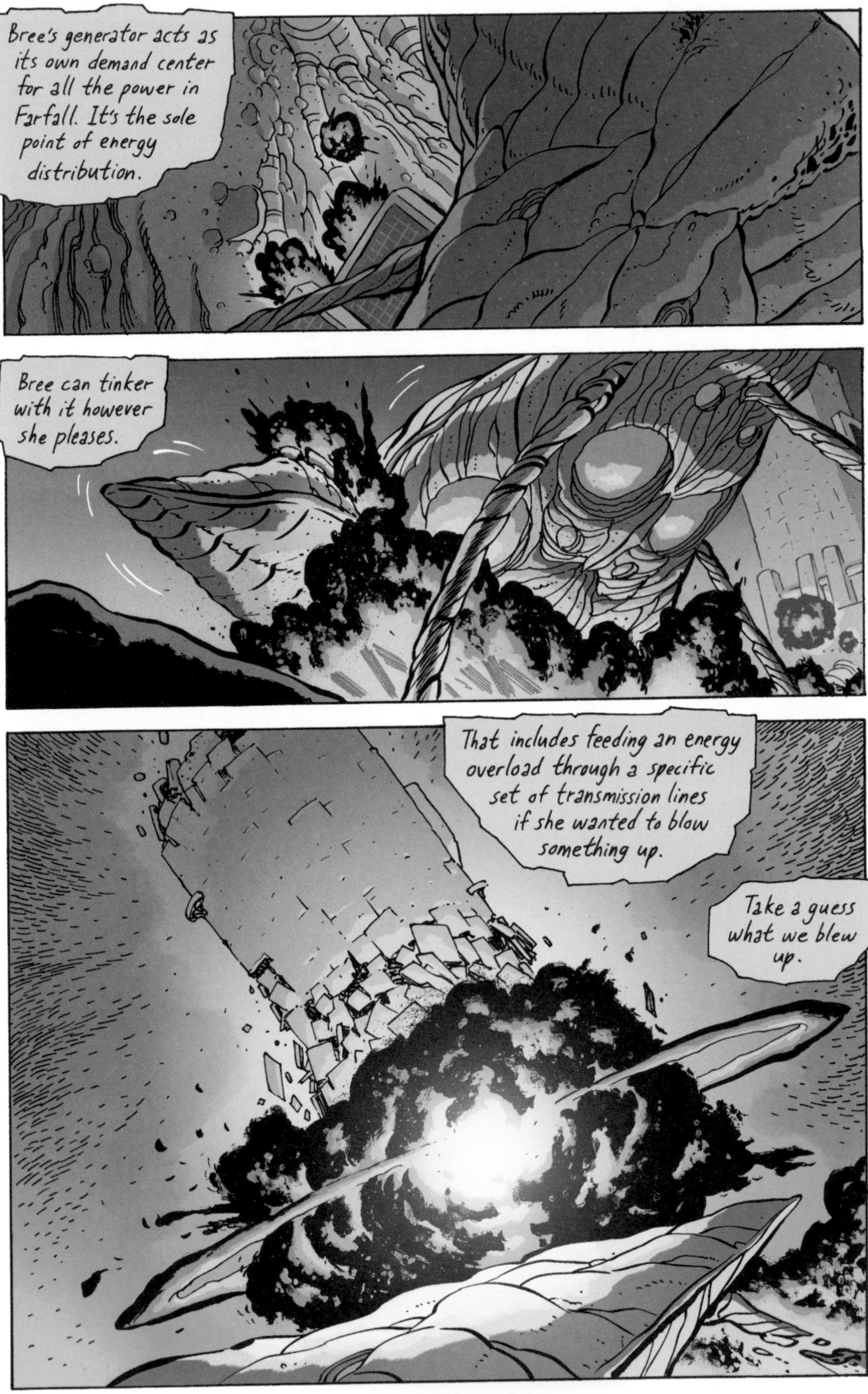
Bree's generator acts as its own demand center for all the power in Farfall. It's the sole point of energy distribution.
Bree can tinker with it however she pleases.
That includes feeding an energy overload through a specific set of transmission lines if she wanted to blow something up.
Take a guess what we blew up.

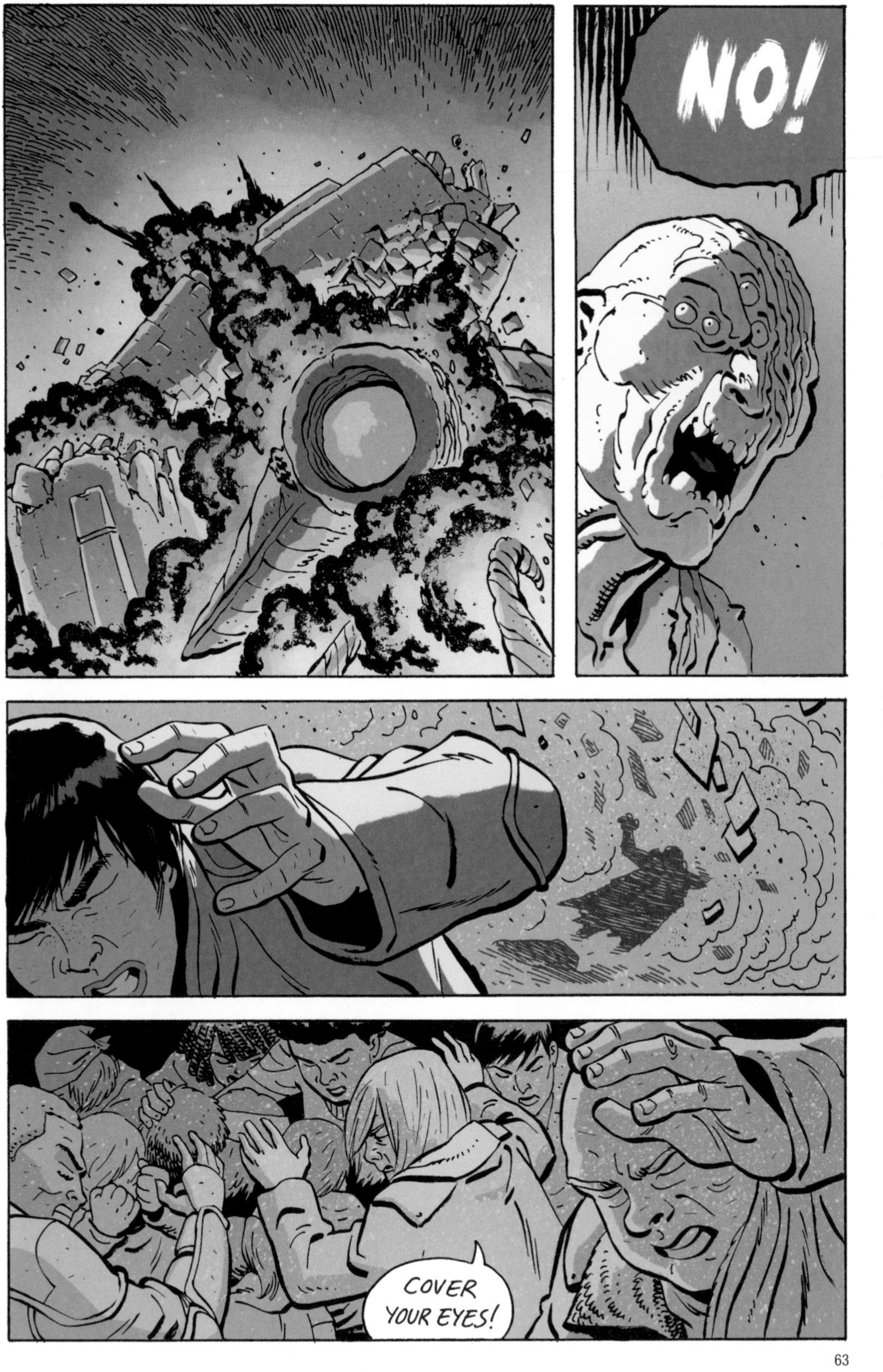
NO!
COVER YOUR EYES!

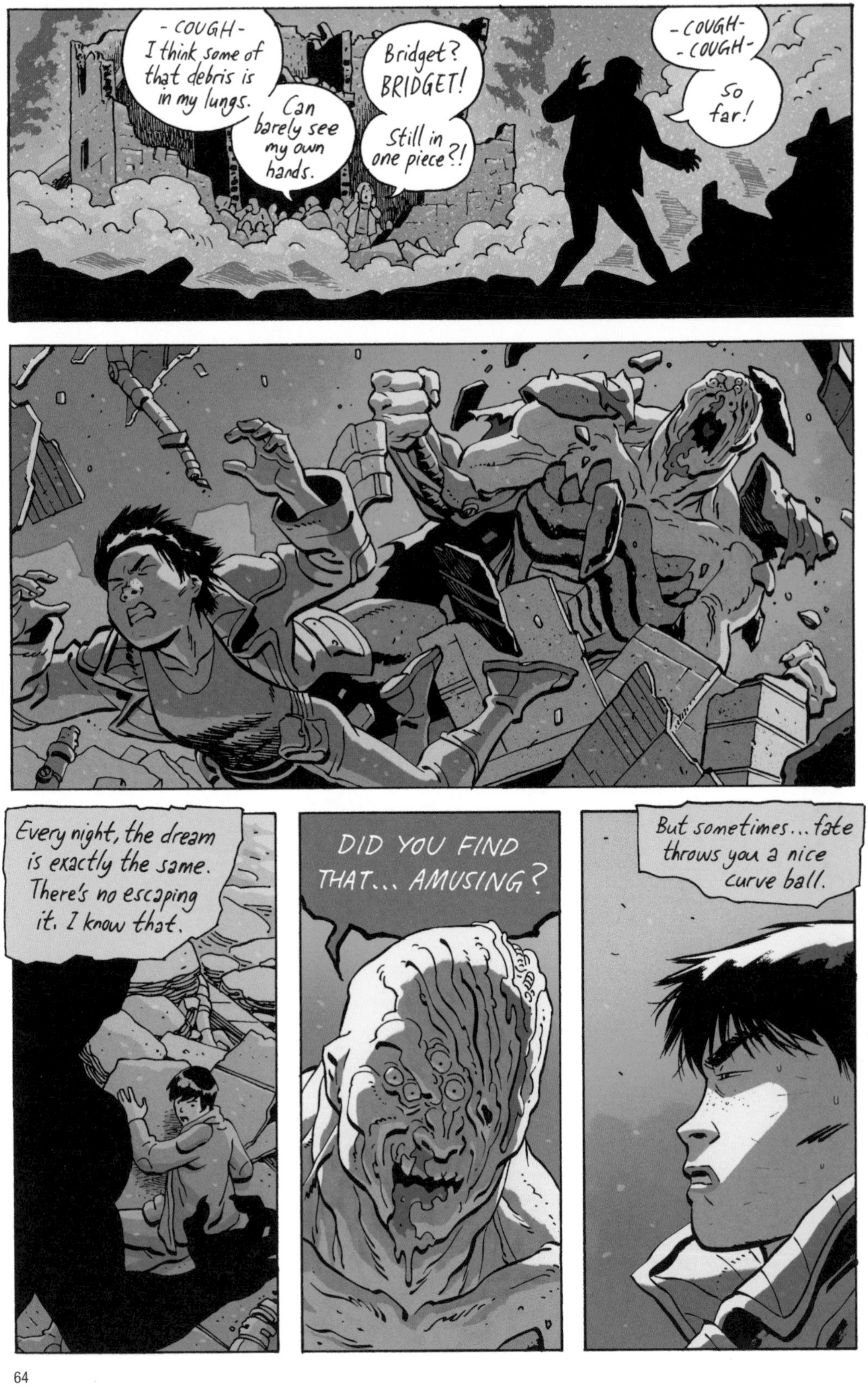
- COUGH - I think some of that debris is in my lungs.
Can barely see my own hands.
Bridget? BRIDGET!
Still in one piece?!
-COUGH- -COUGH-
So far!
Every night, the dream is exactly the same. There's no escaping it. I know that.
DID YOU FIND THAT... AMUSING?
But sometimes... fate throws you a nice curve ball.

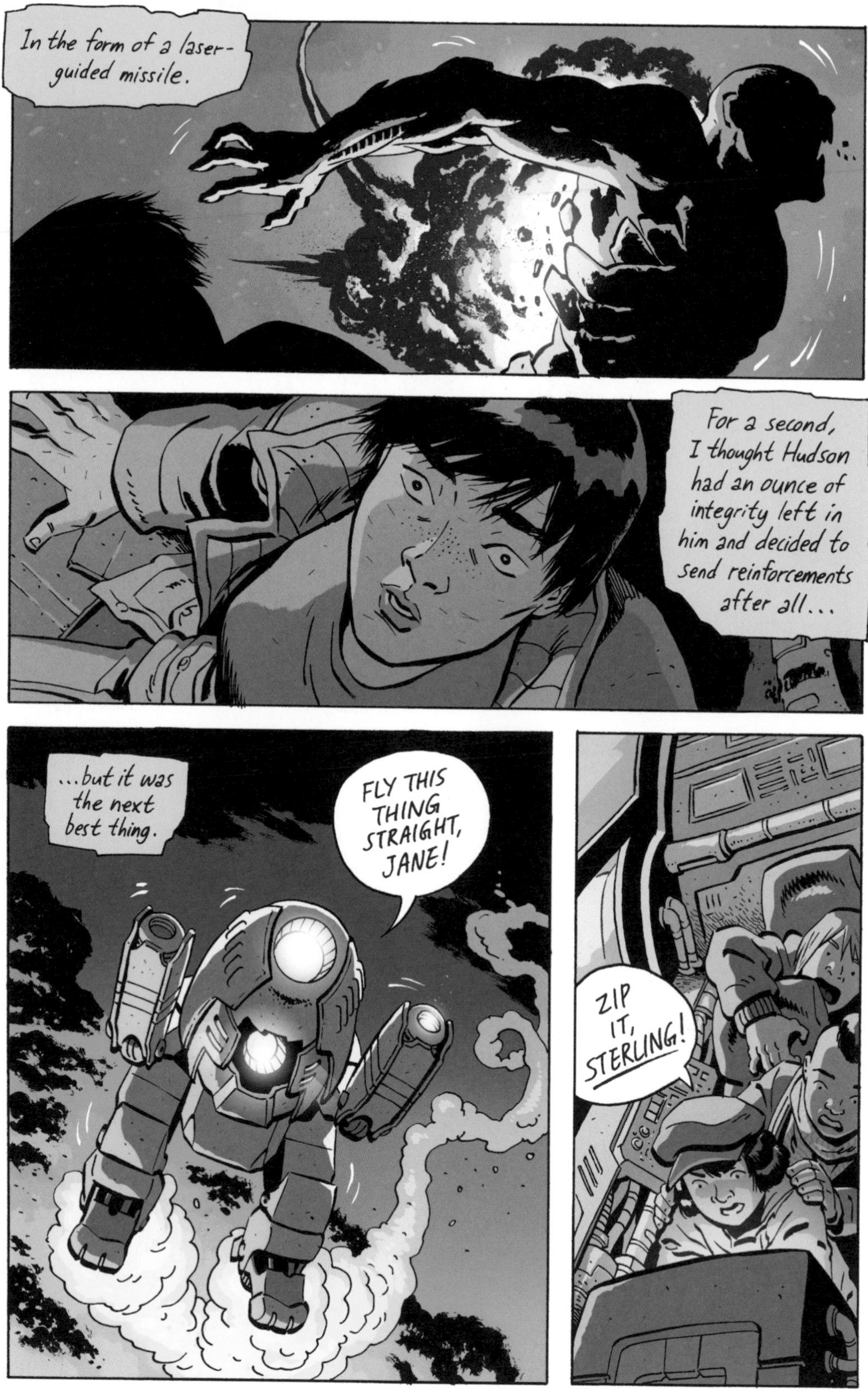
In the form of a laser-guided missile.
For a second, I thought Hudson had an ounce of integrity left in him and decided to send reinforcements after all...
...but it was the next best thing.
FLY THIS THING STRAIGHT, JANE!
ZIP IT, STERLING!

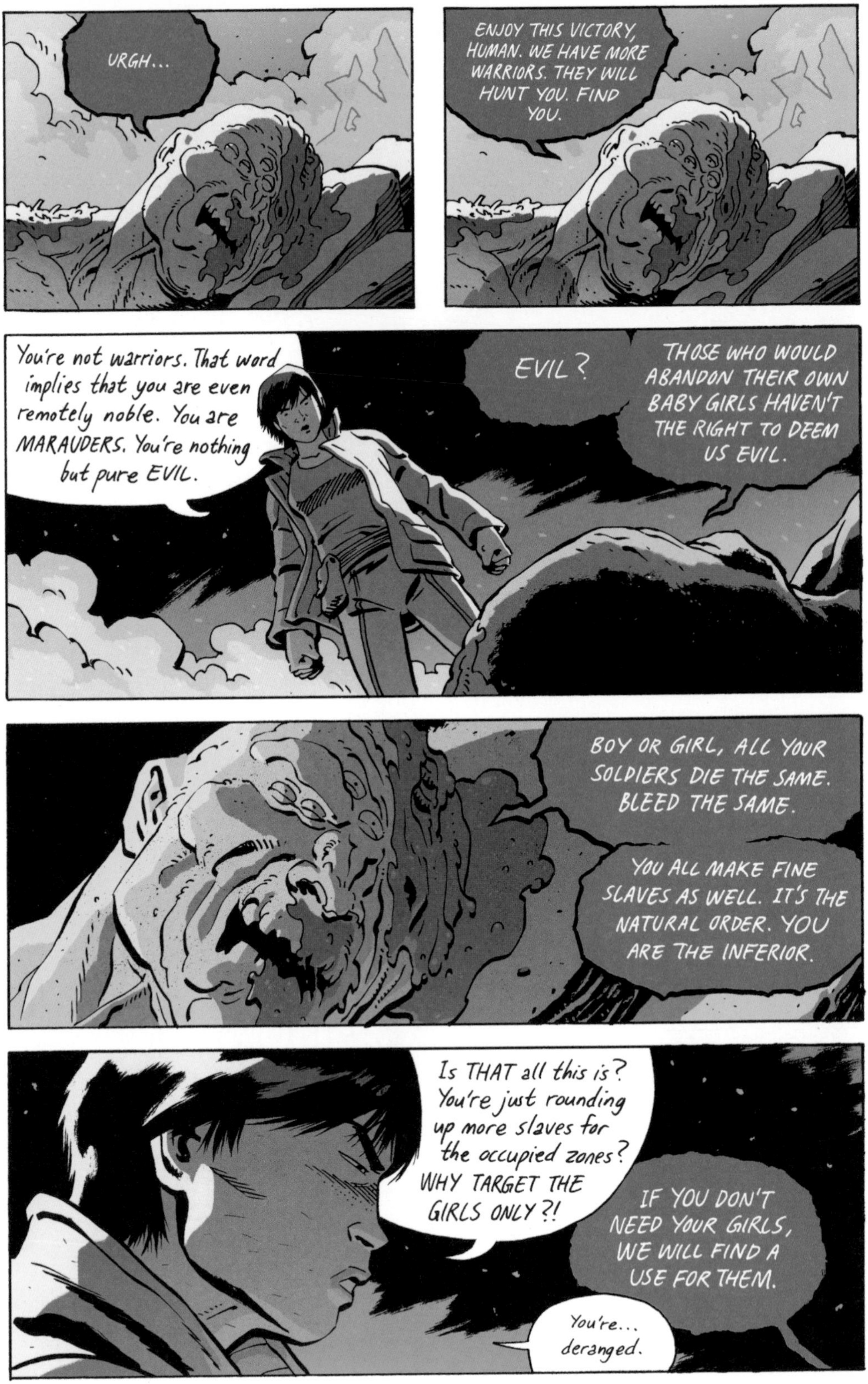
URGH...
ENJOY THIS VICTORY, HUMAN. WE HAVE MORE WARRIORS. THEY WILL HUNT YOU. FIND YOU.
You're not warriors. That word implies that you are even remotely noble. You are MARAUDERS. You're nothing but pure EVIL.
EVIL?
THOSE WHO WOULD ABANDON THEIR OWN BABY GIRLS HAVEN'T THE RIGHT TO DEEM US EVIL.
BOY OR GIRL, ALL YOUR SOLDIERS DIE THE SAME. BLEED THE SAME.
YOU ALL MAKE FINE SLAVES AS WELL. IT'S THE NATURAL ORDER. YOU ARE THE INFERIOR.
Is THAT all this is? You're just rounding up more slaves for the occupied zones? WHY TARGET THE GIRLS ONLY?!
IF YOU DON'T NEED YOUR GIRLS, WE WILL FIND A USE FOR THEM.
You're... deranged.

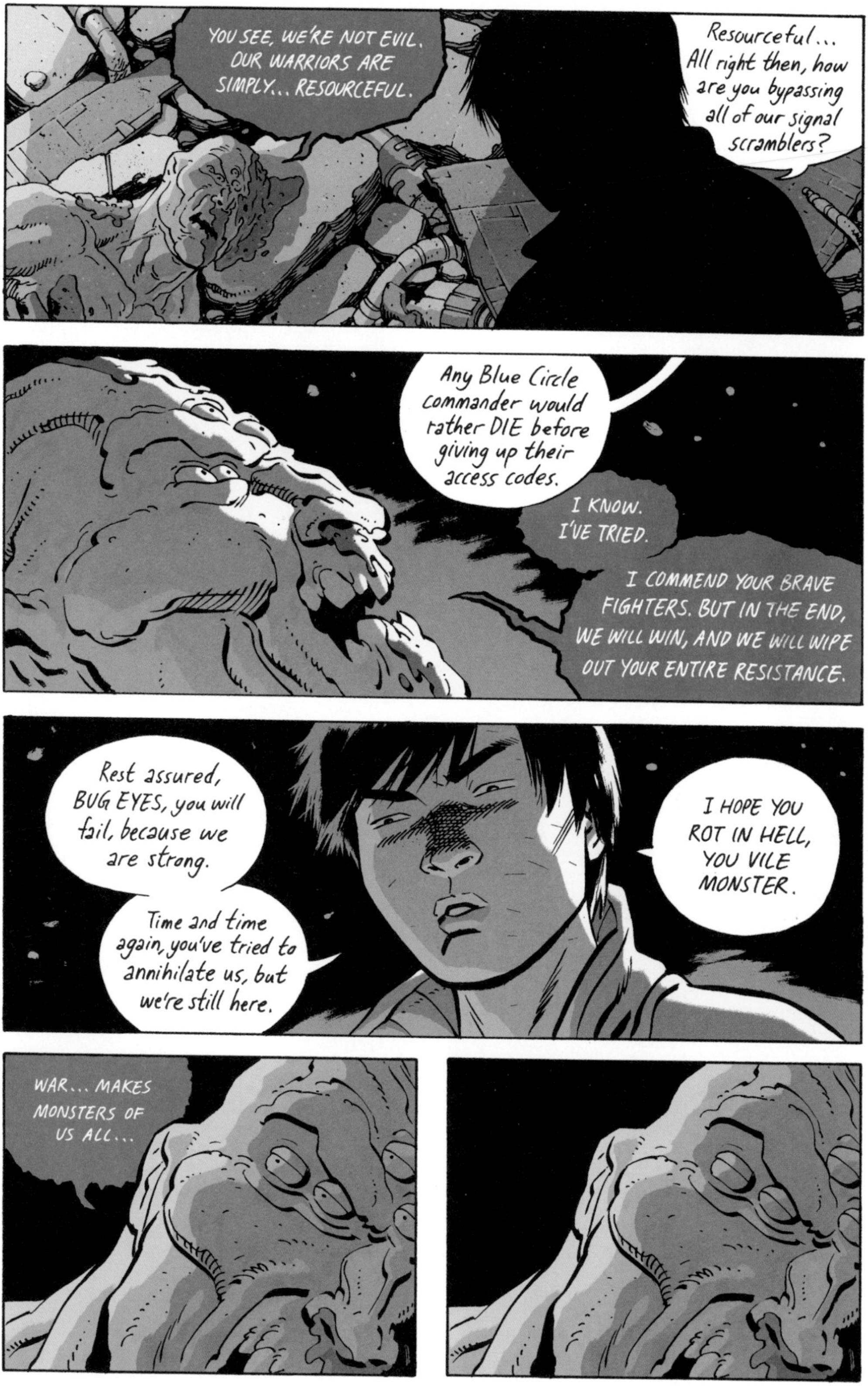
YOU SEE, WE'RE NOT EVIL. OUR WARRIORS ARE SIMPLY... RESOURCEFUL.
Resourceful... All right then, how are you bypassing all of our signal scramblers?
Any Blue Circle commander would rather DIE before giving up their access codes.
I KNOW. I'VE TRIED.
I COMMEND YOUR BRAVE FIGHTERS. BUT IN THE END, WE WILL WIN, AND WE WILL WIPE OUT YOUR ENTIRE RESISTANCE.
Rest assured, BUG EYES, you will fail, because we are strong.
Time and time again, you've tried to annihilate us, but we're still here.
I HOPE YOU ROT IN HELL, YOU VILE MONSTER.
WAR... MAKES MONSTERS OF US ALL...

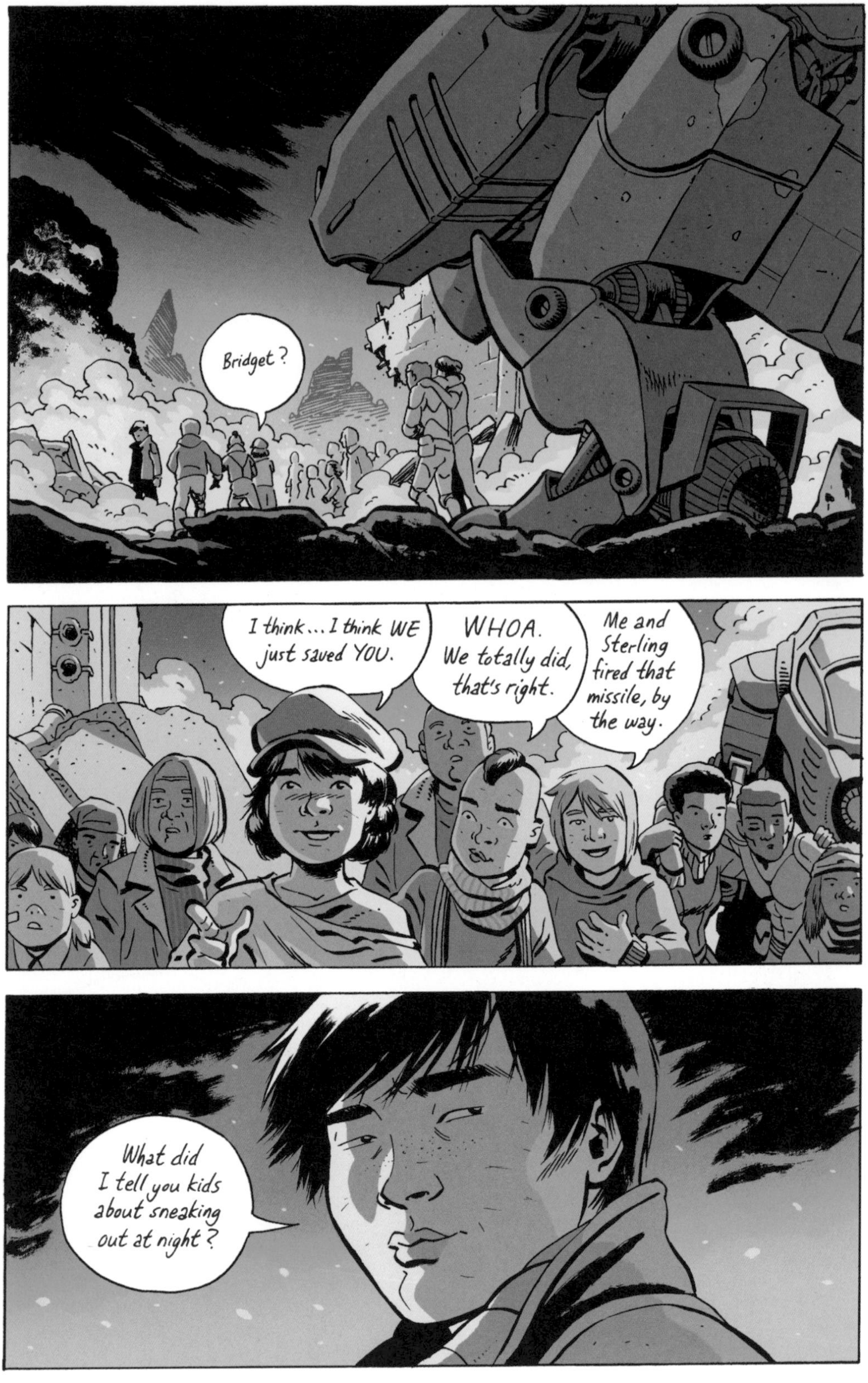
Bridget?
I think... I think WE just saved YOU.
WHOA. We totally did, that's right.
Me and Sterling fired that missile, by the way.
What did I tell you kids about sneaking out at night?

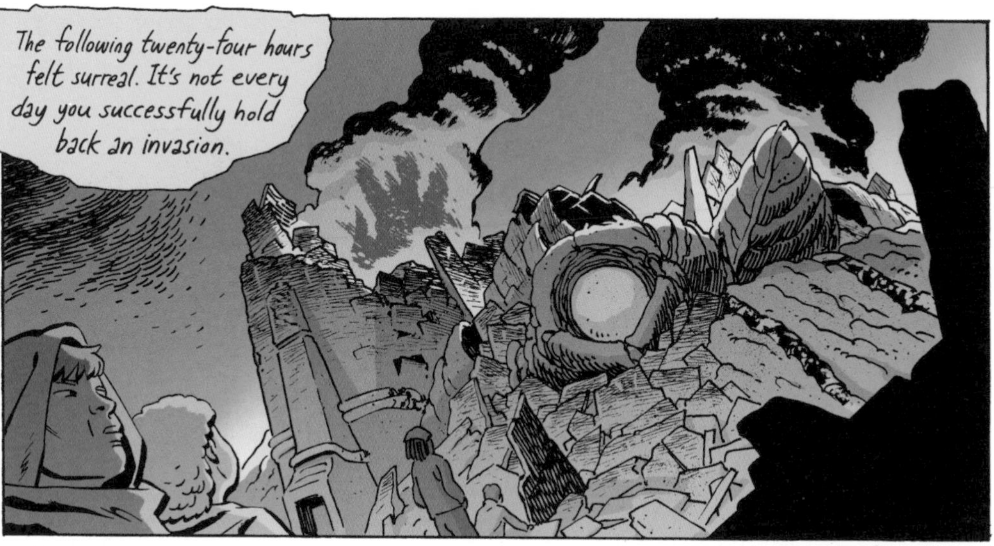
The following twenty-four hours felt surreal. It's not every day you successfully hold back an invasion.

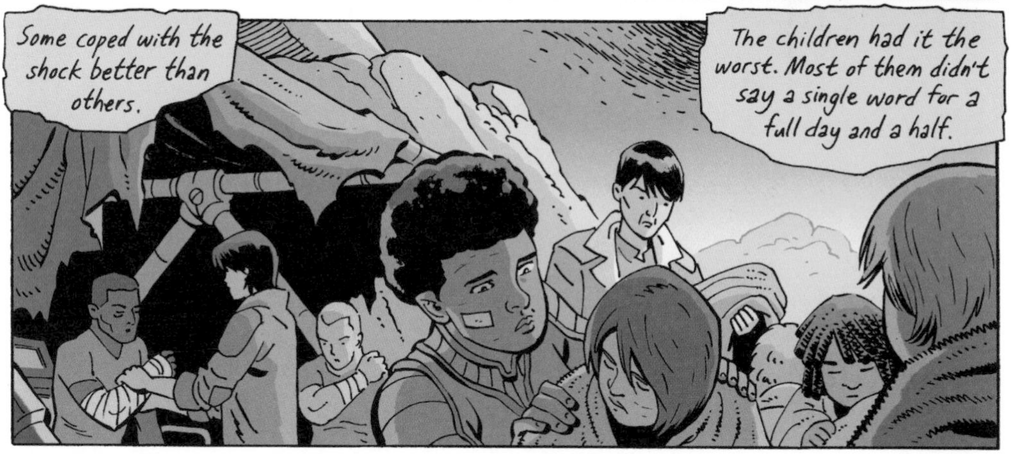
Some coped with the shock better than others.
The children had it the worst. Most of them didn't say a single word for a full day and a half.

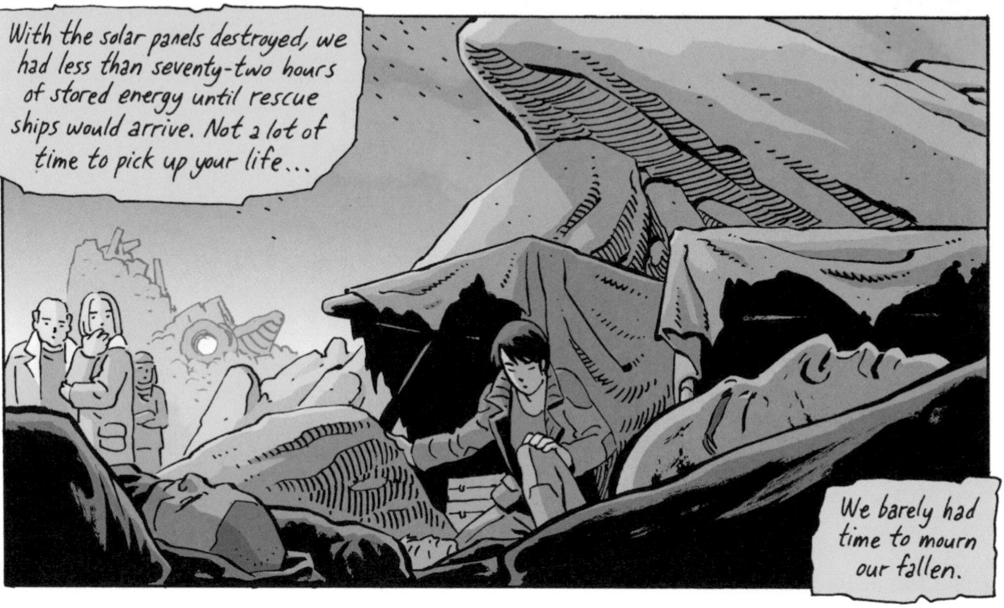
With the solar panels destroyed, we had less than seventy-two hours of stored energy until rescue ships would arrive. Not a lot of time to pick up your life...
We barely had time to mourn our fallen.

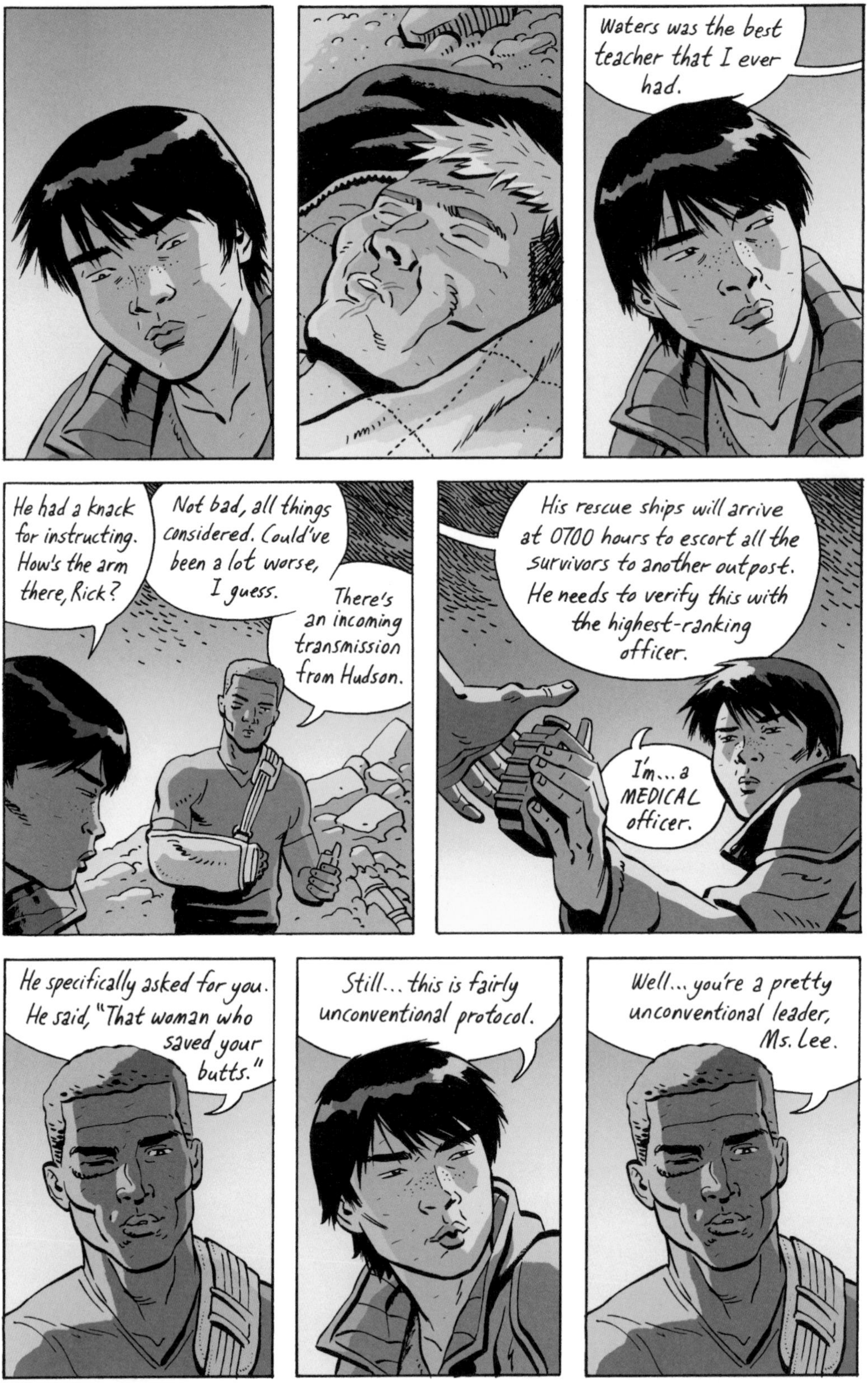
Waters was the best teacher that I ever had.
He had a knack for instructing. How's the arm there, Rick?
Not bad, all things considered. Could've been a lot worse, I guess.
There's an incoming transmission from Hudson.
His rescue ships will arrive at 0700 hours to escort all the survivors to another outpost. He needs to verify this with the highest-ranking officer.
I'm... a MEDICAL officer.
He specifically asked for you. He said, "That woman who saved your butts."
Still... this is fairly unconventional protocol.
Well... you're a pretty unconventional leader, Ms. Lee.

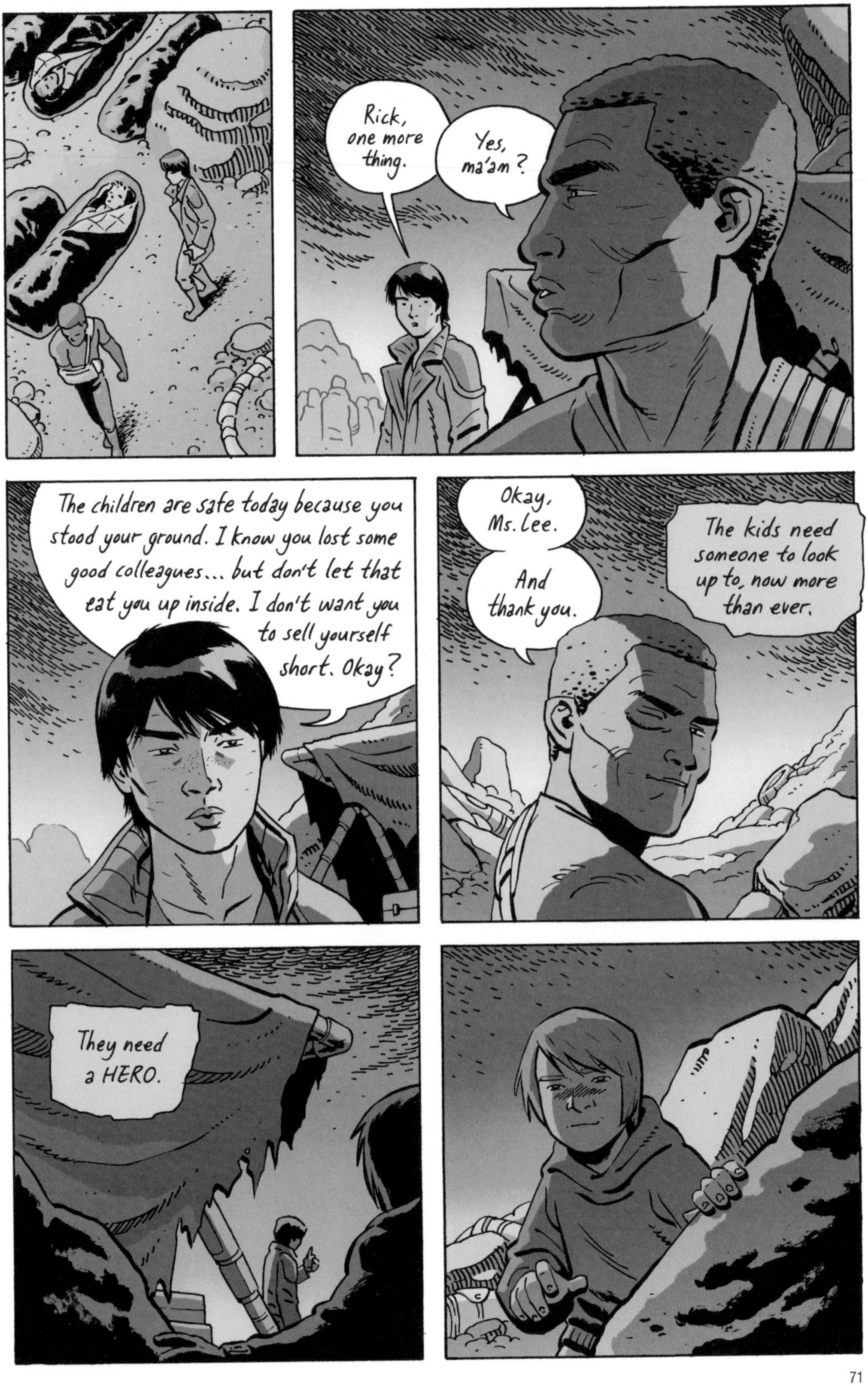
Rick, one more thing.
Yes, ma'am?
The children are safe today because you stood your ground. I know you lost some good colleagues... but don't let that eat you up inside. I don't want you to sell yourself short. Okay?
Okay, Ms. Lee.
And thank you.
The kids need someone to look up to, now more than ever.
They need a HERO.

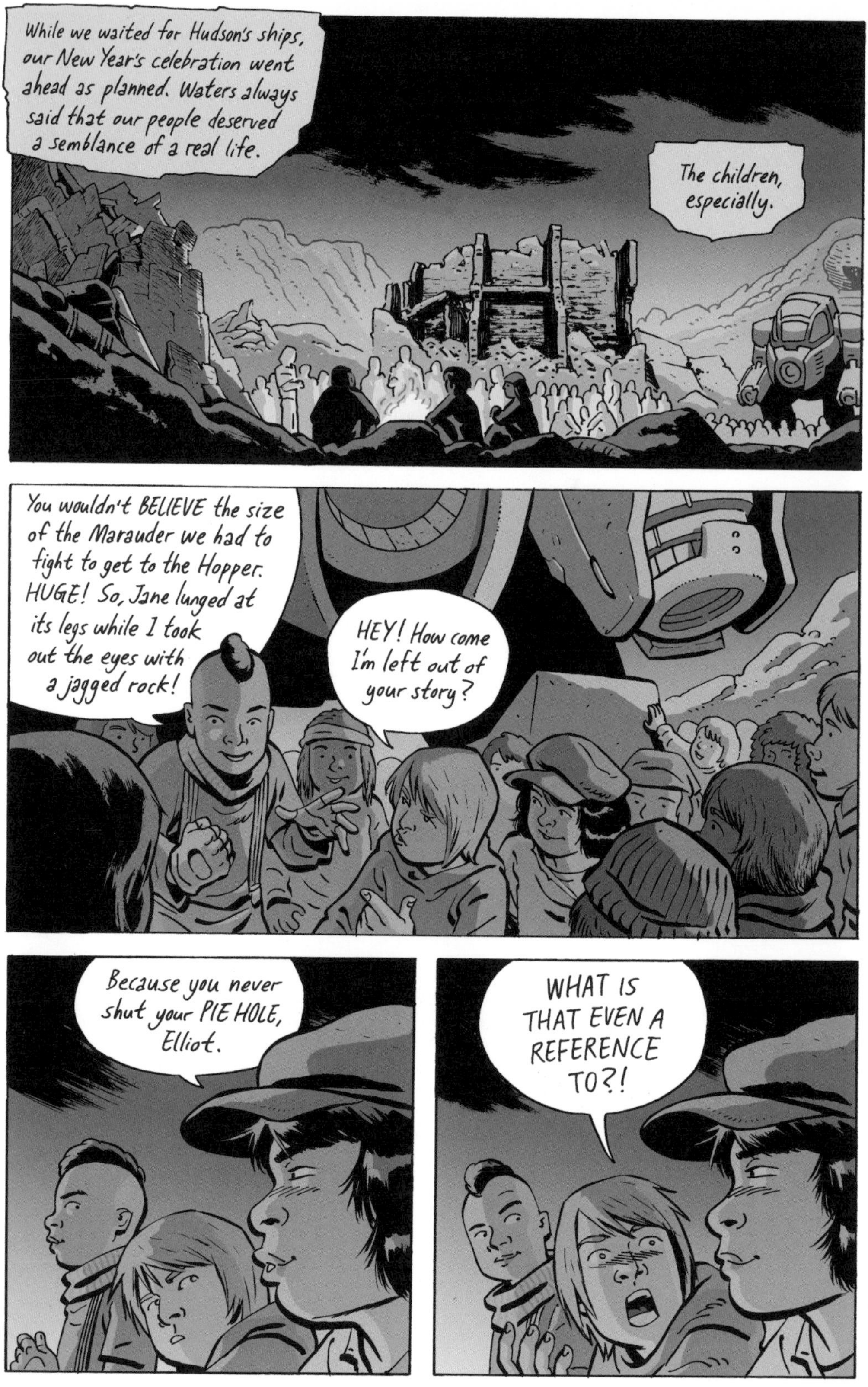
While we waited for Hudson's ships, our New Year's celebration went ahead as planned. Waters always said that our people deserved a semblance of a real life.
The children, especially.
You wouldn't BELIEVE the size of the Marauder we had to fight to get to the Hopper. HUGE! So, Jane lunged at its legs while I took out the eyes with a jagged rock!
HEY! How come I'm left out of your story?
Because you never shut your PIE HOLE, Elliot.
WHAT IS THAT EVEN A REFERENCE TO?!

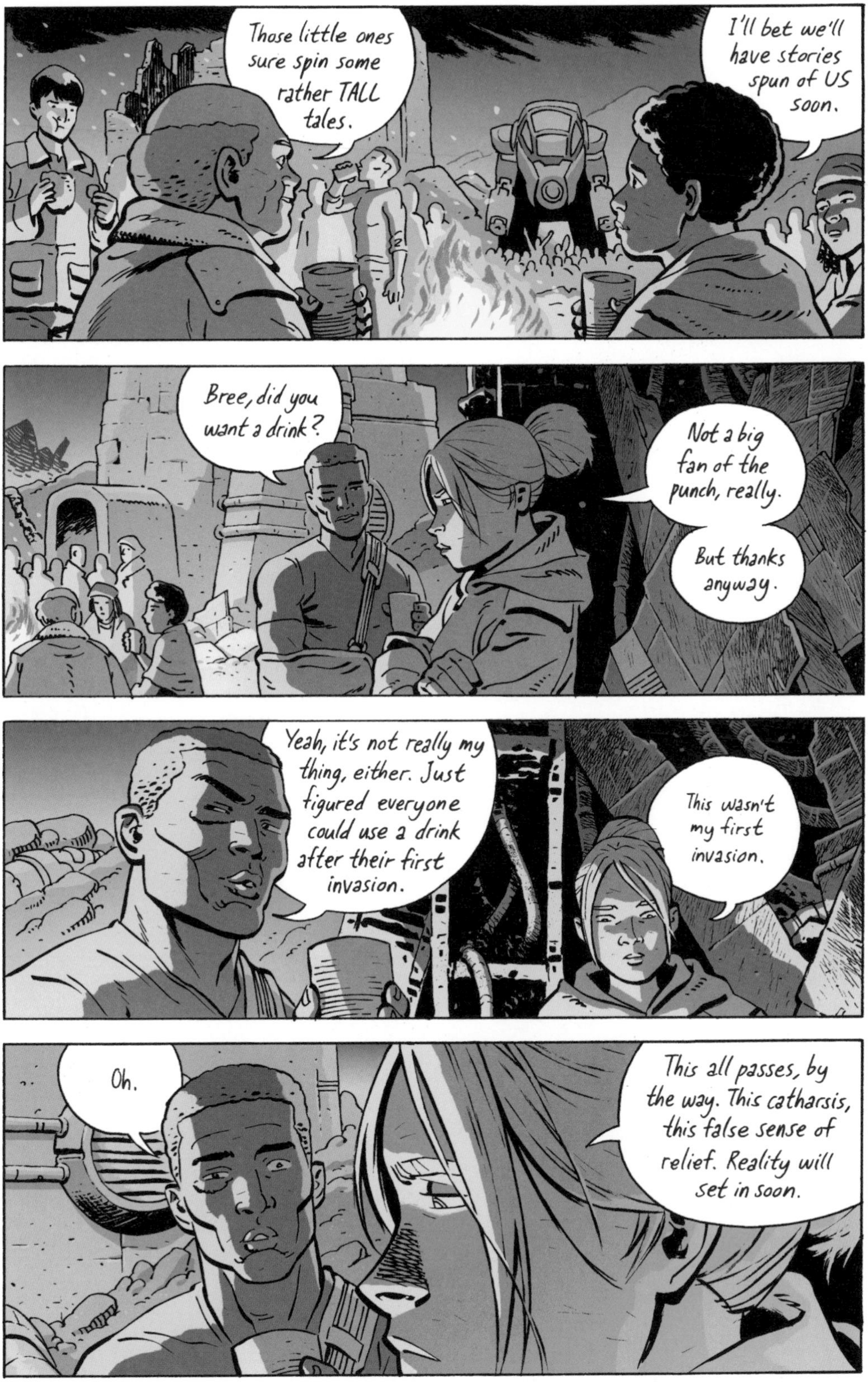
Those little ones sure spin some rather TALL tales.
I'll bet we'll have stories spun of US soon.
Bree, did you want a drink?
Not a big fan of the punch, really.
But thanks anyway.
Yeah, it's not really my thing, either. Just figured everyone could use a drink after their first invasion.
This wasn't my first invasion.
Oh.
This all passes, by the way. This catharsis, this false sense of relief. Reality will set in soon.

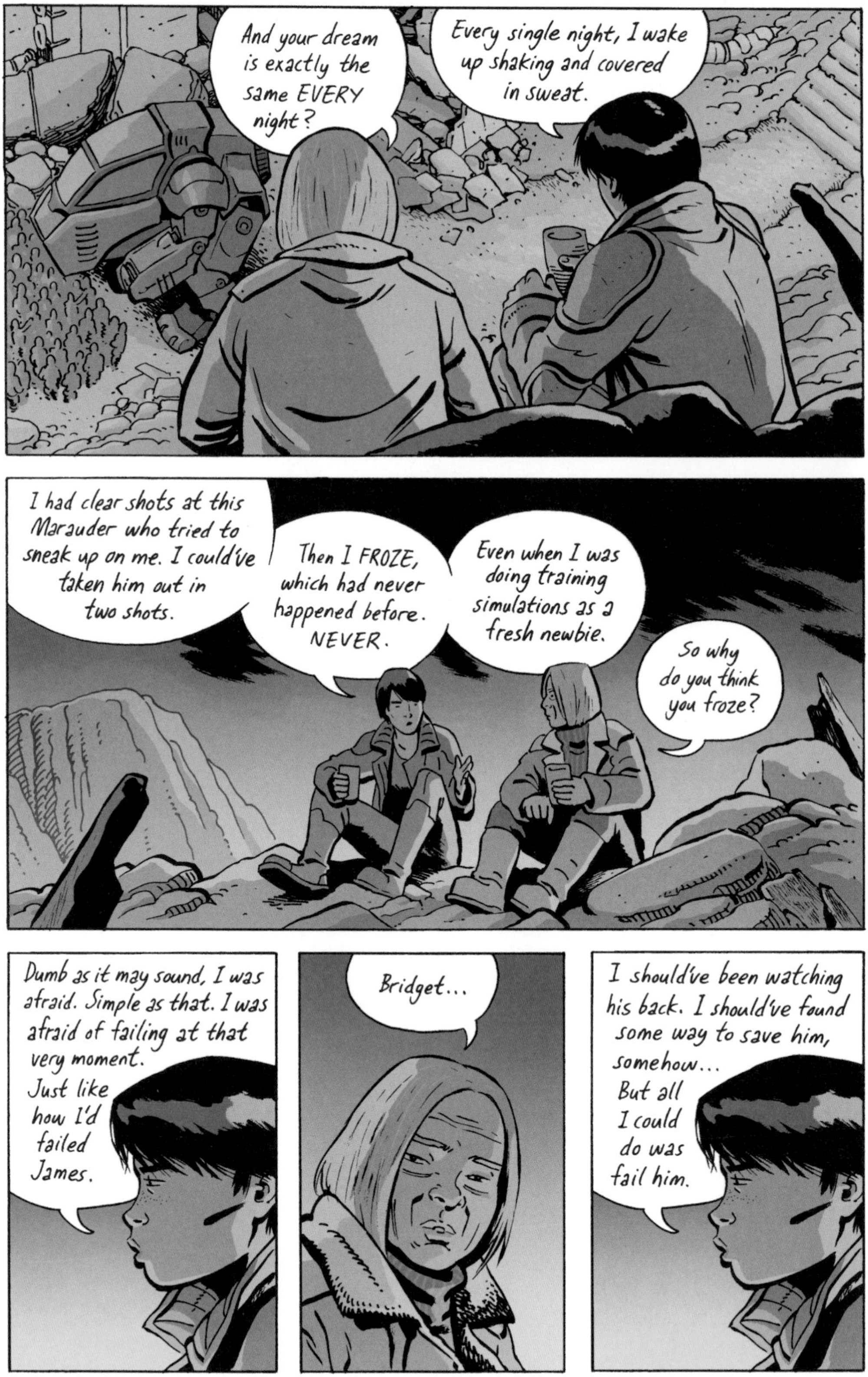
And your dream is exactly the same EVERY night?
Every single night, I wake up shaking and covered in sweat.
I had clear shots at this Marauder who tried to sneak up on me. I could've taken him out in two shots.
Then I FROZE, which had never happened before. NEVER.
Even when I was doing training simulations as a fresh newbie.
So why do you think you froze?
Dumb as it may sound, I was afraid. Simple as that. I was afraid of failing at that very moment. Just like how I'd failed James.
Bridget...
I should've been watching his back. I should've found some way to save him, somehow... But all I could do was fail him.

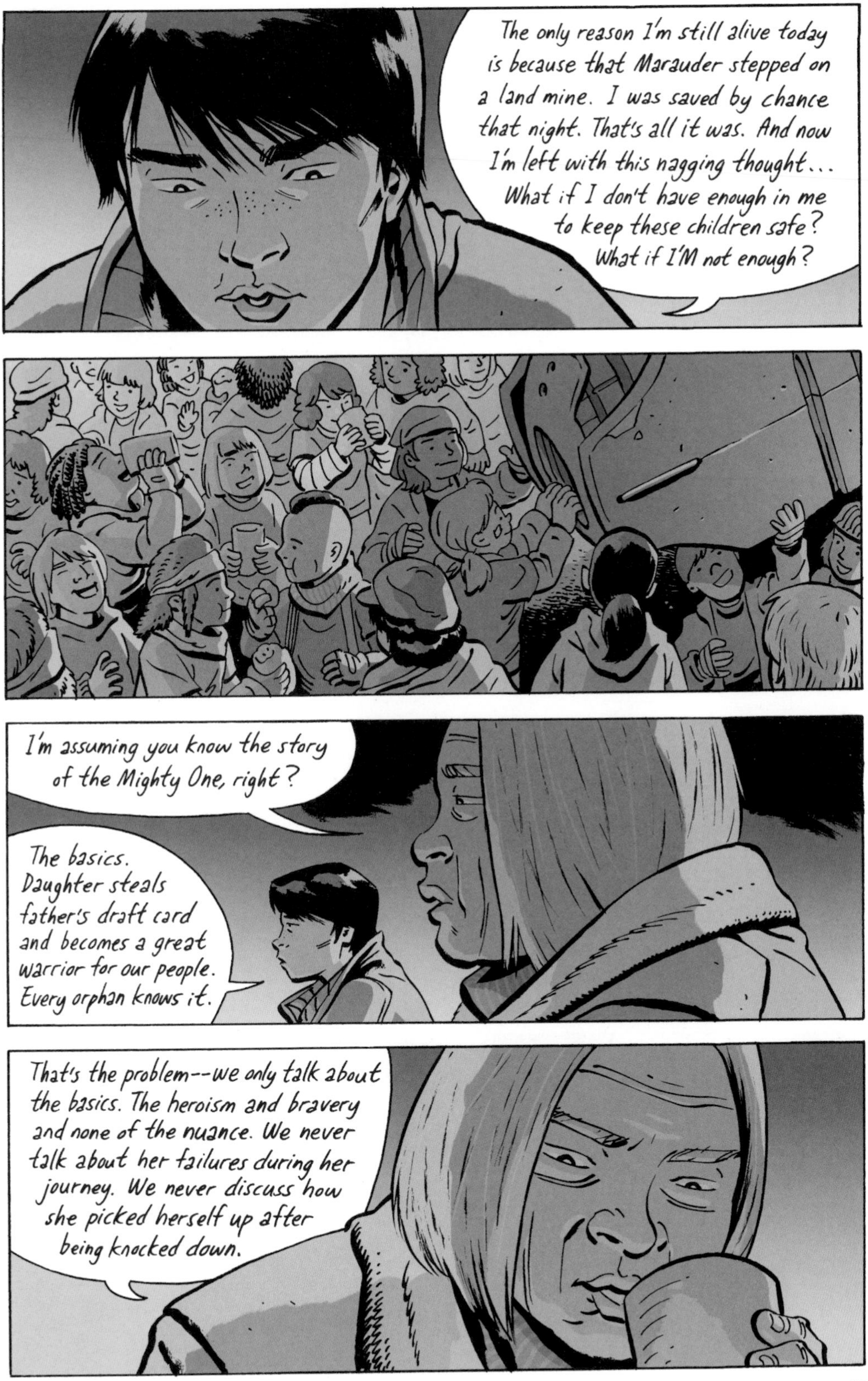
The only reason I'm still alive today is because that Marauder stepped on a land mine. I was saved by chance that night. That's all it was. And now I'm left with this nagging thought... What if I don't have enough in me to keep these children safe? What if I'M not enough?
I'm assuming you know the story of the Mighty One, right?
The basics. Daughter steals father's draft card and becomes a great warrior for our people. Every orphan knows it.
That's the problem--we only talk about the basics. The heroism and bravery and none of the nuance. We never talk about her failures during her journey. We never discuss how she picked herself up after being knocked down.

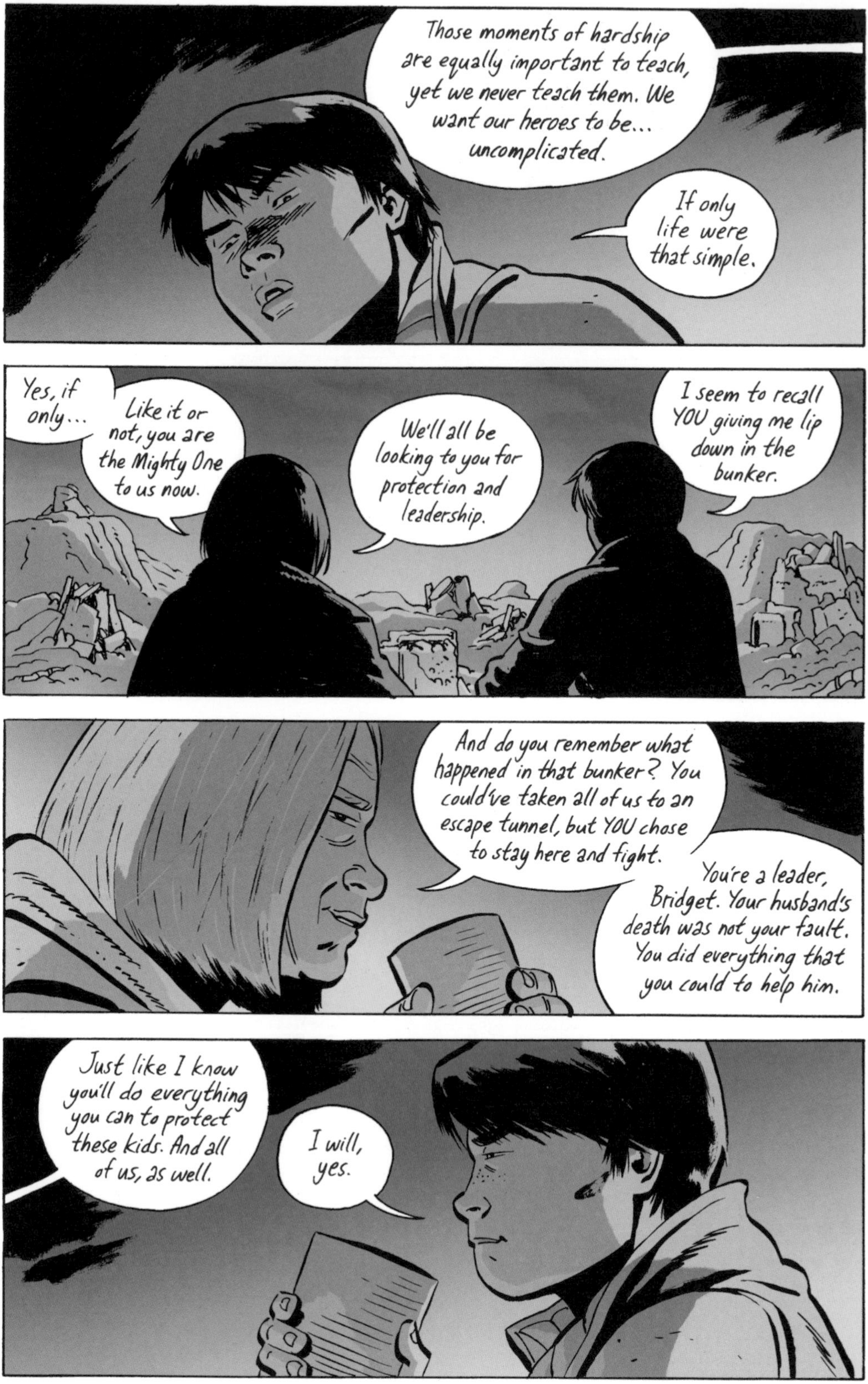
Those moments of hardship are equally important to teach, yet we never teach them. We want our heroes to be... uncomplicated.
If only life were that simple.
Yes, if only...
Like it or not, you are the Mighty One to us now.
We'll all be looking to you for protection and leadership.
I seem to recall YOU giving me lip down in the bunker.
And do you remember what happened in that bunker? You could've taken all of us to an escape tunnel, but YOU chose to stay here and fight.
You're a leader, Bridget. Your husband's death was not your fault. You did everything that you could to help him.
Just like I know you'll do everything you can to protect these kids. And all of us, as well.
I will, yes.

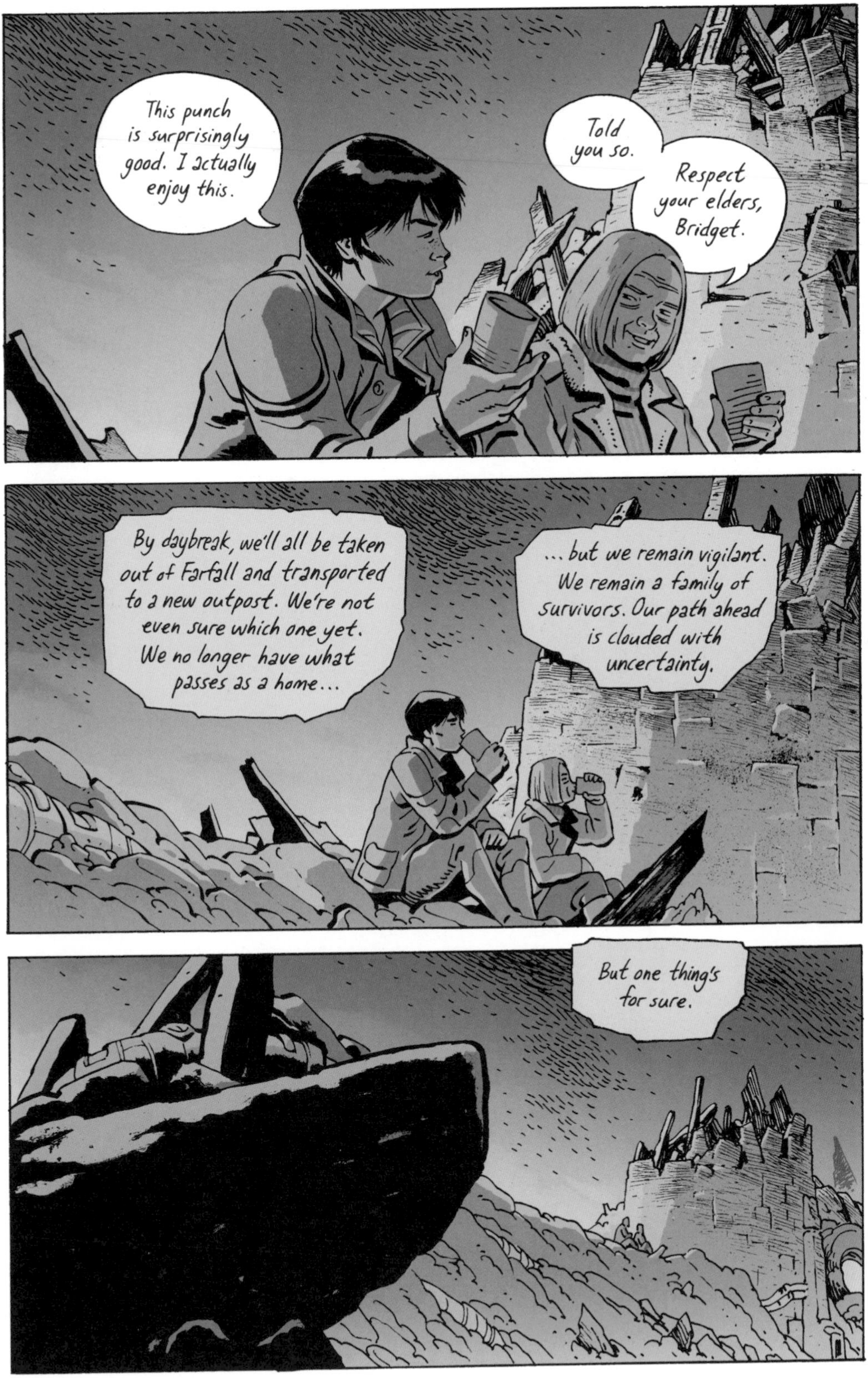
This punch is surprisingly good. I actually enjoy this.
Told you so.
Respect your elders, Bridget.
By daybreak, we'll all be taken out of Farfall and transported to a new outpost. We're not even sure which one yet. We no longer have what passes as a home...
...but we remain vigilant. We remain a family of survivors. Our path ahead is clouded with uncertainty.
But one thing's for sure.

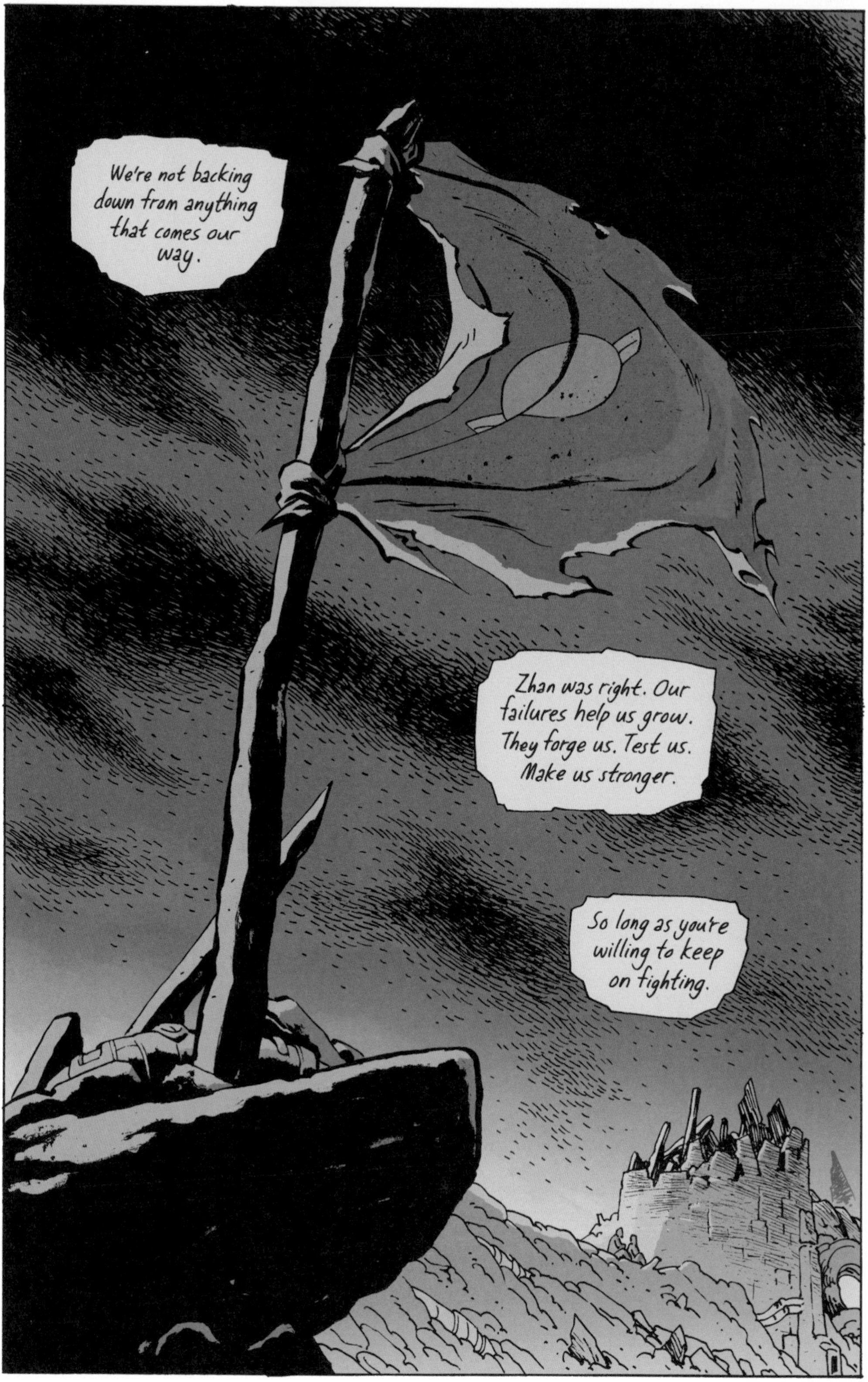
We're not backing down from anything that comes our way.
Zhan was right. Our failures help us grow. They forge us. Test us. Make us stronger.
So long as you're willing to keep on fighting.

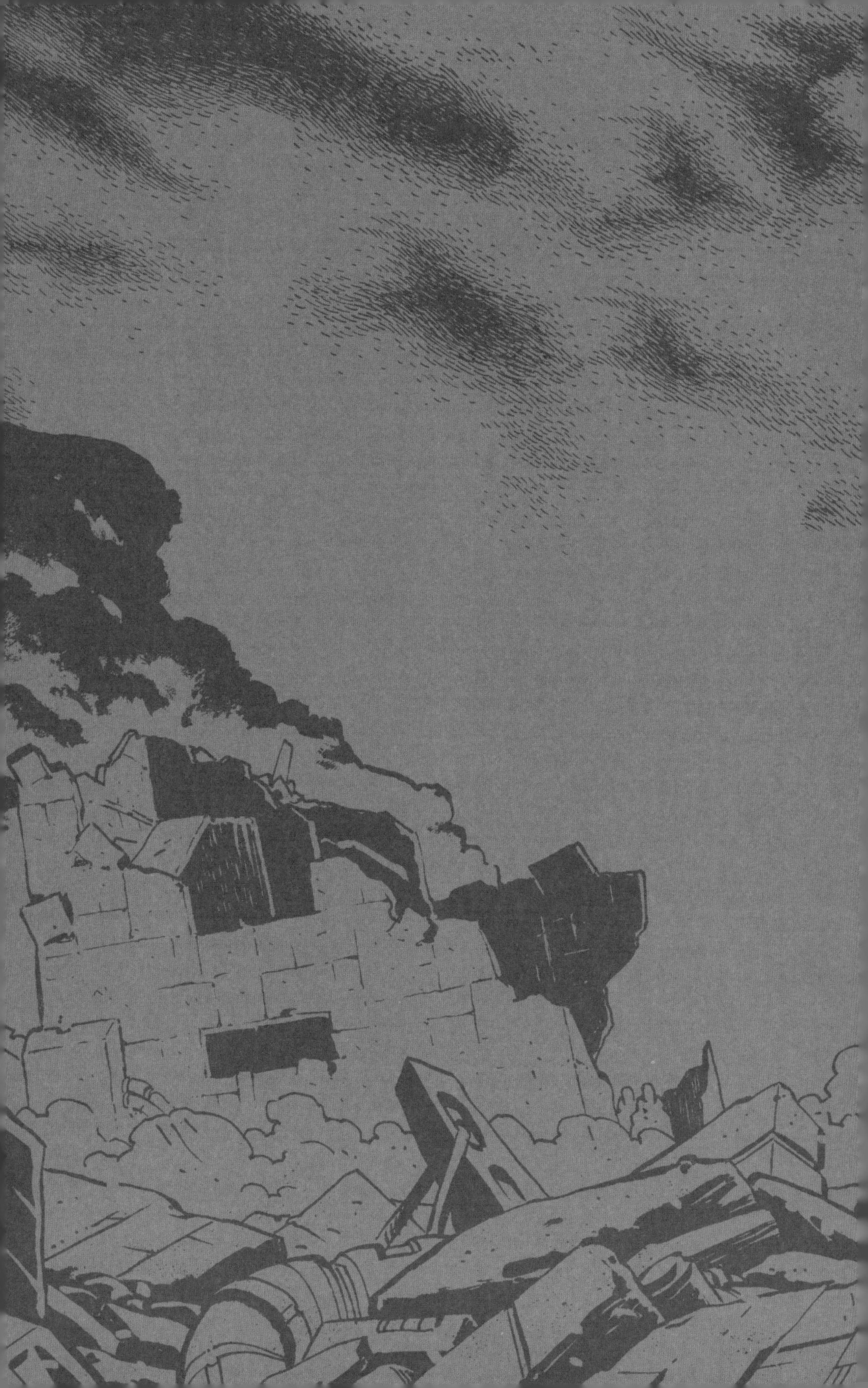

MORE FROM AWARD-WINNING CREATOR

# ETHAN YOUNG

*"Young's style is fresh and accessible . . . His eye for striking single panel compositions [and] his layouts and pacing are memorable." —The Beat*

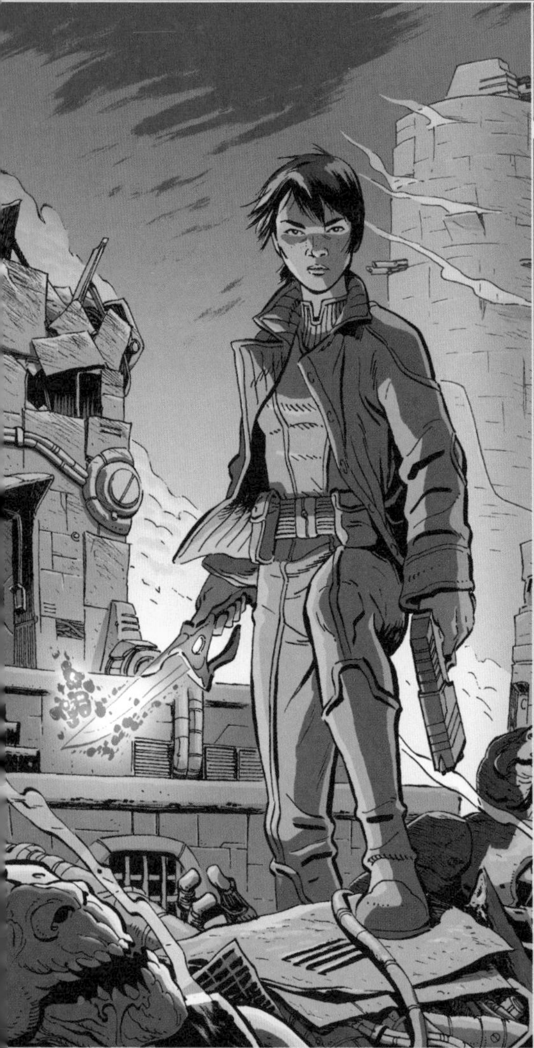

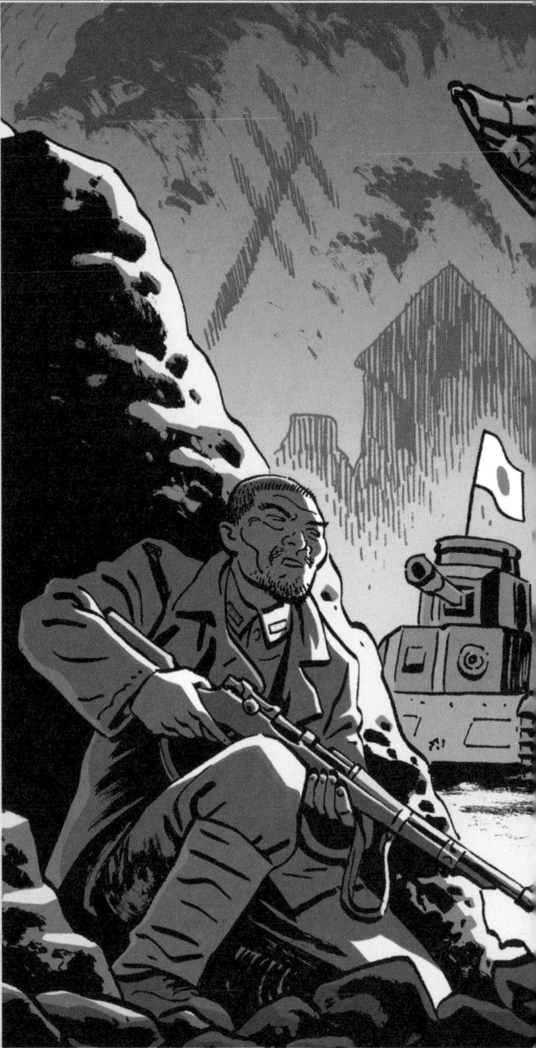

## THE BATTLES OF BRIDGET LEE: INVASION OF FARFALL

There is no longer a generation that remembers a time before the Marauders invaded Earth. Bridget Lee, an ex–combat medic now residing at the outpost Farfall, may be the world's last hope. But Bridget will need to overcome her own fears before she can save her people. Her legend begins here.

ISBN 978-1-50670-012-0 | $10.99

## NANJING: THE BURNING CITY

After the bombs fall, the Imperial Japanese Army seized the Chinese capital of Nanjing. Now screams echo off the rubble as two abandoned Chinese soldiers—trapped and desperately outnumbered inside the walled city—try to escape. What they'll encounter will haunt them. But in the face of horror, they'll learn that resistance and bravery cannot be destroyed.

ISBN 978-1-61655-752-2 | $24.99

**AVAILABLE AT YOUR LOCAL COMICS SHOP OR BOOKSTORE!** • To find a comics shop in your area, call 1-888-266-4226.
For more information or to order direct—On the web: DarkHorse.com | Email: mailorder@darkhorse.com | Phone: 1-800-862-0052
Mon.–Fri. 9 AM to 5 PM Pacific Time.